FORGIVE

AND MOVE ON

A CHRISTIAN GUIDE TO FORGIVING OTHERS

MICHAEL A. WILSON

TRILOGY

Trilogy Christian Publishers
A Wholly Owned Subsidary of Trinity Broadcasting Network
2442 Michelle Drive
Tustin, CA 92780
Copyright © 2019 by Michael A. Wilson
All Scripture quotations, unless otherwise noted, taken from THE
HOLY BIBLE, NEW INTERNATIONAL VERSION®, NIV® Copyright © 1973, 1978, 1984, 2011 by Biblica, Inc.® Used by permission. All rights reserved worldwide.
Scripture quotations marked (NIV) taken from The Holy Bible,
New International Version. Cambridge Edition: 1769.

For information, address Trilogy Christian Publishing
Rights Department, 2442 Michelle Drive, Tustin, Ca 92780.
Trilogy Christian Publishing/ TBN and colophon are trademarks of
Trinity Broadcasting Network.
For information about special discounts for bulk purchases, please
contact Trilogy Christian Publishing.
Manufactured in the United States of America

Trilogy Disclaimer: The views and content expressed in this book
are those of the author and may not necessarily reflect the views
and doctrine of Trilogy Christian Publishing or the Trinity Broadcasting Network.

Cover illustration: Michele Keren Stitt, Artist/Designer

10 9 8 7 6 5 4 3 2 1
Library of Congress Cataloging-in-Publication Data is available.
ISBN 978-1-64088-896-8
ISBN 978-1-64088-897-5

This book is dedicated to my family and those who've had to persevere. God still has a plan for your life, and you can get back up again!

Acknowledgments

Thank You,

—Rev. James and Diane "Ma" Wilson (parents), Rachel (wife), Jordan, and Jayda (daughters), James Jr. and Michele (brother and sister), Rev. Claggett and Mrs. Sheila Ward (in-laws), Sisters-In-Law (Debbie, Chrissy, Michele, and Kim), countless aunts (including Linda, Janette, Pat, Bell, Dorothy, Anne, and Veronica), uncles (including Arthur and Moses), cousins, nieces, nephews, grandparents (Dorothy, James, Jobie, John, and Marguerite).

—The Redeemed Christian Worship Center family, Fort Foote Baptist Church, From the Heart Church Ministries, Bishop Aubrey and Mrs. Jeri Farrar, Rod "Lil Bro" Shuler, Mr. James "J.B." Brown, Dr. John Cherry I (late), Dr. Tony Evans, Dr. Myles Munroe, Dr. E.V. Hill, Mr. Carl "Kokayi" Walker, Mr. Tony E. Michener (late), Rev. Bruce (late) and Mrs. Brenda Haliburton, "Ma" Viola Wilson (late), Dr. Delores Smith (late), Mr. Calvin Hampton, Sis. Lori G. Ellis (adopted sister), Mr. Malcolm Jackson, Sis. Dorona Chappelle, Sis. Mary Jenkins, Sis. Cas-

sandra Fooks, Min. Sharon, and Mr. Josh Calloway..
—The Beach Family, the Stubblefield Family, the Wright Family, Min. Thomas and Doris Brown, the Clark Family, the Leigh Family, the Holmes Family, the VanBrakle Family, Mr. Derrick Staton, Mr. Rodney Staton, Sis. Ada and Kids, Elder Luis and Dr. Mildred Catarineau, Mr. Gary Coltrane, Luis and Marcella Catarineau.
—Pastor Joseph W. Lyles, Pastor Kevin Gross, Pastor Douglas Wilson, Pastor Calvin Smith, Pastor Tremaine Davis, Pastors Daniel and Sabrina Mangrum, Rev. Jerry Falwell Sr. (late), Min Anthony McCollum (late) and Rev. Jesse L. Jackson. Michele Keren Stitt for the illustration inspiration and artwork.
—Special thank you to my new TBN, Trilogy books family.

Table of Contents

Preface

It is possible that you are reading this book and have no earthly idea of what it truly means for you to forgive others. Like a lot of things in life, we can successfully tell people what to do but cannot explain how to do it. Forgiveness is one of those things that is attached to quick quips and prose by preachers, counselors, and motivational speakers. However, how do we do it?

This book will examine one of the most overstated actions that we are encouraged to take in schools, churches, mosques, and synagogues: to forgive. It's time to dream big again, enjoy your life, and end your anxiety about ever seeing the person that you can't forgive.

One of the challenges with forgiving others is that we keep allowing people back into our lives that will repeatedly hurt us! If you're ready to live again, then this book will inspire you to do so while looking at simple principles and biblical examples to exercise your own personal resolve. We will explore together why we are not healed and, once and for all, you will forgive and rise up to live again!

1.

Moving into Healing
Being Made Whole

Mark 5:25-28

In 1989, when I met the late E.V. Hill, pastor of one of the largest black congregations in the United States, I was so impressed with his directness and ability to align himself with several different types of people. I was one of many people who showed up to hear Dr. Hill speak during a three-night seminar, and I immediately became a big fan from a distance.

In the 1960s, Dr. Hill was a confidant of Dr. Martin Luther King and a founding member of the Southern Christian Leadership Council. In the 1980s, Dr. Hill was both a supporter of Jesse Jackson and Ronald Reagan. Therefore, having met Jackson as a teenager in high school, where I shared the same stage and microphone, Dr. Hill was alright with me!

At the end of Dr. Hill's address to 20,000 people in a crammed college auditorium one night, I stood in line to meet him. I had hopes of becoming his newfound pen pal or, at the very least, learn more about his political views and world travels. However, I was immediately discarded with an abrupt handshake and a quick side-step so he could proceed on to the next hand in line.

At that moment, I was thinking about what it was like to be dissed by this old civil rights preacher. My thoughts about him were not good. I felt it was his responsibility to encourage young people and not discourage them. Now, I can only imagine there are many of you reading this chapter who have had a similar experience and have felt the same way before.

In turn, I didn't have godly thoughts because I couldn't believe this old preacher from Los Angeles would practically stiff-arm a young fan of his. Even worse, I couldn't understand why his abrasiveness affected me enough to care about this limited interaction I had experienced with him. Knowing that he was speaking again the following night, I began to question if I should even give him the respect and attend, even though I already committed myself to come to this event.

Later that night when I returned home, I couldn't even tell anyone about what had happened, except for my roommate and mother. My roommate didn't understand what I was explaining to him, but my mother was full of encouragement. My mother didn't want this silly moment to define me, so she supported the idea of me going back the next night to hear him speak again.

I laid awake that night pondering if I should go back. I was also trying to figure out why his actions meant something to me. I guess there was a little hero worshiping on my end towards Dr. Hill, and this is how God cures us of this: He lets people let you down! After thinking about what my mother had said to me about this situation, I was still unsure if I should go back the next night.

The next day during class, all I could think about was being stiff-armed from the night before. I couldn't concentrate on the instructor, and nothing was making sense to me. My mind was completely focused on one person—Dr. Hill. Even after class, I couldn't eat without seeing his big, beady eyes; the eyes I was only able to see as he swiftly brushed past me to take the time to talk to others. This lackluster interaction replayed over and over and over again. Every moment I was reminded of being dissed by this big, burly man whom I looked up to.

That evening, I decided to attend his seminar again to hear him speak. As I approached the colosseum, my stomach became queasy. Once inside, I found my place. As I read the opening title of his message, *You Can Go to Hell*, I once again had thoughts about Dr. Hill that I do not care to share!

As soon as the program started, I began feeling trapped in my seat among 20,000 people and forced to listen to him speak. While sitting there, though, I had planned on letting him out of my heart and mind. Although I was only a young adult in college, I had seen before what it was like for someone to have a person lodged in their heart affecting their ability to eat, sleep, and/or function normally. I was not about to allow this experience of having someone lodged in my heart in that way, especially if he didn't mean to do it.

For the next forty-five minutes, I was unimpressed with him and his message. My stomach was churning, and my teeth were clenched. I kept asking God to help me until it didn't matter how I felt. I knew it wasn't about me anyway, but about whatever I was supposed to experience from the message that night. Besides, he couldn't see me staring back at him amongst the humongous crowd. He couldn't hear my inner thoughts and what I thought he should do. He couldn't feel my pain and probably didn't even know what he had done to me. My pain was from a distance, and now I needed my forgiveness to be from a distance in my own time.

As I sat there, I decided that blocking out the speaker and missing what he had to say was not worth it anymore. Why give up my joy and excitement in life over something like this? I decided to let it go, and when I did, I could finally hear his words and listen attentively. I didn't bring up the negative feelings from the night before. Something broke inside of me, and it didn't make sense, but more importantly, I was free... I thought.

Racing across my mind and in my heart was the need to speak to him again. *Oh, snap!* I thought. Why was this encounter all of a sudden so important to me? I didn't know. I couldn't remember if my mother put me up to this, but my heart was now pounding as his message came to an end, and everyone stood up applauding. I found myself walking forward to join the same line where I was hurt the first night. This time, with a lower expectation of him and greater expectations of myself, I decided to go up to him and tell him that I had forgiven him. This world-class traveler, a remnant of the 60s, a friend of Dr. King and Rev. Billy Graham, was about to hear me tell him that I forgave him.

My goal was to approach Dr. Hill, drop the forgiveness word on him, and keep moving through the line, but I found myself telling him the whole story from when I approached him the night before up until approaching him at that moment. With no malice, fear, disappointment, anger, rejection, or trepidation, I told Dr. Hill, "and... I forgive you."

At the end of my story, Dr. Hill's big hands grabbed my shoulders. As he sized me up and looked me in the eyes, he said, "You forgive me? Well, all is well, isn't it?" There was no emotion on my part, just the satiety of being heard and telling him that I released him. I had given up my rejection and disappointment to the point that it really didn't matter if he heard me. I had let the man go, and that was enough for me. I was satisfied with my decision to tell him about my experience and that I had forgiven him.

On February 24, 2003, Dr. Hill passed away, and thousands mourned his death and celebrated his life at his funeral. I had one encounter with him that left me hurt and another one right after I choose to forgive because it is possible one can never see a person again and still be hurt. It is also highly possible to continue to see a person who's hurt us and choose to be healed. I was healed up in the stands

7

while sitting with 20,000 people, and my healing happened from a distance.

Healing should be the goal for anyone who's hurt and what healing really means when it comes to forgiveness is wholeness. However, how often do we miss the goal of wholeness in our lives because we're carrying around an unforgiving heart? Like me, it is so easy for you to begin to collect the things people have done that hurt you and not maintain your wholeness. Although I was only a young adult at that time, I knew that carrying around hurt from someone whom I didn't know personally was going to cause me to miss a greater quality of life.

You Have to Want Wholeness

In Matthew, chapter 9, there was a certain woman who had a blood disease. While her goal was to become "whole" physically, she also suffered spiritually because of others. Since she is a great example of what wholeness is, we cannot ignore her pursuit of a more abundant life. It is possible to be a Christian, love Jesus, and be somehow stagnate in your personal growth in God. If you are not careful, complacency can turn into apathy, which can turn into becoming spiritually arthritic, meaning you stop growing spiritually as a person.

Oftentimes, a difference between your life and someone else's can come down to a dream being deferred due to the issues of one's heart. My all-time favorite movie and play, *A Raisin in the Sun*, was adapted by Lorraine Hansberry based on a poem entitled *Harlem*, also known as a *Dream Deferred*, by the late Langston Hughes. In his poem, Hughes writes, *"What happens to a dream deferred? Does it dry up like a raisin in the sun?"* ("Harlem by Langston Hughes" 2019). Are you a person whose dreams are deferred and dried up like a raisin in the sun because of unforgiveness? Don't you want to be made whole?

Most of the time, we blame not reaching our full potential on other people. However, when you blame people, you empower them. Furthermore, most people who don't reach their full potential or follow their destiny aren't always the most unfortunate ones either. All you have to do is become a bitter or angry person because of what someone has done to you, and you will end up sending out negative signals to everyone and everything that is around you.

Because unforgiving people are usually the most misinformed people in terms of who they are and what they are about, they stunt their growth. They fail to pull up the weeds of unforgiveness that surround their lives, which keeps them from growing. Your neighborhood, education, color, size, weight, IQ, relationship status, or the number of children you have to take care of by yourself are not the real reasons why many of us do not reach our potential and wholeness of life. Harboring unforgiveness usually robs us of the riches of an abundant life.

"Being confident of this very thing, that he which hath begun a good work in you will perform it until the day of Jesus Christ" (Philippians 1:6, KJV).

This means that God is working on all of us, but we cannot put all the work of becoming whole on God. The thing that pushes us from our present frustration into our future situation is a revelation from God!

In Mark, chapter 5, there were three people who Jesus came in contact with and in need of healing: a young man who was being demonized, a father whose daughter was deceased, and a woman who was diseased.

In the early part of chapter 5, there is a **young man** who was delivered from **demons.** In the end part of chapter 5, there is a **young girl** who was delivered from **death.** However, in between these two miracles, was a **yearning woman** who was terribly stricken with a **disease** and what she was up against in getting better was three things.

First, no one could help her rid herself of her disease. This relates to the idea that sometimes no one can help you. "And had suffered many things of many physicians..." (Mark 5:26, KJV). This woman sought after many doctors. Doctor after doctor tried to help her, but none of them could. Whenever you're trying to become whole and drop unforgiveness, no one can help you get over it. This is a journey of recovery you're on by yourself! Haven't you realized by now that no one is going to come along, lift unforgiveness from you, and give you wholeness? As much as you love the people around you, and they love you as well, unforgiveness is an unwanted gift you return to the sender!

Second, her situation became worse over time.

This passage continues with, "...and had spent all that she had, and was nothing bettered, but rather grew worse" (Mark 5:26, KJV). It is possible that while you are reading this book, your situation between you and another person has become worse, even though you may have sought outside help. What do you do when your arguing goes to fighting? When the sickness unforgiveness turns into the disease of an angry heart? Don't think that time or some automatic thing will just happen, and you will forgive the person. An unchecked heart of unforgiveness always has the potential to become worse.

Finally, she was known for her problem, not for who she really was. No one knew her real name. "And a certain woman, which had an issue of blood twelve years" (Mark 5:25, KJV). This woman is nameless to us because she is all of us. She becomes known for her problem. A "woman" was who she was, but an "issue of blood" was what she had. If you're not careful, then you will become known as the person who is unforgiving to others. You are being known for your problem, not for who you are. People around you will know that if they cross you, you will have a hard time letting it go.

Are You in Your Own Way?

What do you do when people associate your problem with you as a person? It's almost unfair to call one by their problem, but our heart of unforgivingness is something that others can see and will talk about without ever telling us that they see it. **Therefore, this is one of the reasons why**

11

you need to free yourself from bondage before people start associating you with your problem. This woman in the Bible had an issue, but she was not the issue!

In order to grow up in God and move into our destiny, we have to be willing to confront our real issues. The word "issue" here, in Greek, means to flow constantly or nonstop ("Strong's Greek: Issue" 2019). The issue for the woman in the Bible was directly related to her physical issue: uncontrollable hemorrhage. While her real issue in this biblical narrative was her bleeding, it doesn't mean that she didn't have other hang-ups that you and I can relate to when it comes to forgiving others.

Like the woman in this story, we need to be able to do at least two things. First, forgive yourself. "When she had heard of Jesus, came in the press behind..." (Mark 5:27, KJV). This woman approached Jesus from behind because this issue she dealt with caused her embarrassment, disappointment, and probably shame to the point that she felt unworthy for Jesus to see or touch her. She approached Him in secret because she didn't want Jesus to know that it was her—an unclean woman. Also, her seeking doctors and sources other than Jesus may have made her feel bad enough not to want to approach Jesus. Whatever you have done may also plague you even to the point of not wanting to pray or be around people today. You see, the reason why some of us are stuck in trying to reach our destiny is that we can't get past whatever we've done. Have you ever had to forgive... yourself?

Why is it so hard to forgive ourselves? Why do we treat ourselves worse than we treat the devil or other people? Like this woman, unforgiveness of self keeps us from boldly approaching Jesus. Undoubtedly, the trick of the enemy is to make you think that the thing you've done is somehow separating you from the love of God!

Remember:

> For I am persuaded, that neither death, nor life, nor angels, nor principalities, nor powers, nor things present, nor things to come, nor height, nor depth, nor any other creature, shall be able to separate us from the love of God, which is in Christ Jesus our Lord.
>
> (Romans 8:38–39, KJV)

Have you ever held yourself up from your destiny by not forgiving yourself? Have you ever said to yourself, "I don't deserve to be forgiven?" One needs to understand the idea that conviction leads to repentance, repentance leads to reconciliation, and reconciliation leads to restoration. However, accusation and guilt will lead you to shame and self-condemnation.

> There is therefore now no condemnation to them which are in Christ Jesus...
>
> (Romans 8:1, KJV)

After you have cried out to God, He forgives you and holds no record of wrong against you. It's the enemy who wants to keep it in your face, and oftentimes, he uses people to do it. These people will say, "Look at you. Aren't you supposed to be a man or woman of God," or "Who do you think you are? I thought *you* didn't do that kind of thing?" Even better, they will say, "Aren't you a Christian?" Although the devil may use others around you, no condemnation means no condemnation in the eyes of God. God doesn't want you to feel bad about something that has been covered under the blood of Jesus Christ. You have the grace of God operating on your behalf.

The second reason why many people aren't whole and reaching their destiny is they cannot forgive others. "And had suffered many things of many physicians, and had spent all that she had..." (Mark 5:26, KJV). This woman in the Bible had wasted her money on so-called cures. She gave her money away to quacks and alleged healers. I am sure that it didn't make her feel good when she realized that she had thrown away her life savings on what she thought was the answer. She had suffered by the hands of these doctors, and because of these physicians, this woman was subject to cruel and harsh treatments that did not work. Therefore, these doctors were to blame for her not being healed because they promised her healing, but nothing worked for her.

Who do you need to forgive who promised you something, and they did not follow through? Who have you surrendered your keys of happiness and wholeness to?

Honestly, some of you are in bondage due to blaming other people for your bondage and keeping you bound. In your mind, you wouldn't be in this situation if it weren't for them or you wouldn't have this problem if it weren't for them. To begin your forgiveness journey towards wellness, you have to stop saying you are this way because of someone else!

Ultimately, this biblical woman sought help from medical doctors. But instead of healing, they hurt her even more. Likewise, one of the most devastating types of hurt is when church people hurt you because there is no hurt like a church hurt! These people, in our minds, are supposed to know better, but they are just like everyone else. They let you down, hurt your feelings, turn their backs on you, and prove their humanity to us over and over again. However, these are people who supposedly love you, but hurt you instead.

Therefore, I am here to tell you that it's ok because people are just people. If you should become an angry, bitter, blaming person, then you will give the keys to your destiny and wholeness to other people. Nevertheless, if you are going to be healed, then it has to be God helping you with this. To this end, we shouldn't thank people too long who were instrumental in our promotion. Just the same, we shouldn't blame people too long who were instrumental in our demotion. If people can't heal you (that really comes from God), then people cannot harm you (that really comes from the devil). Once you realize that it's the devil, then you also realize that it's time to release others and yourself.

The fact that you are not whole is not your parents' or your brothers' and sisters' fault. Actually, you were marked by the enemy for death when you were born!

> The thief cometh not, but for to steal, and to kill, and to destroy...
>
> (John 10:10, KJV)

It's time to make the devil pay for his part in what happened to you and to forgive people.

How Do You Make the Devil Pay?

- By not becoming what he said about you!
- By not giving into what he tried to do to you!
- By not going down without a fight!

> For the weapons of our warfare are not carnal, but mighty through God to the pulling down of strong holds.
>
> (2 Corinthians 10:4, KJV)

When you realize that it's the devil who has set up those thoughts against you, then you can pull them down. When you realize that it's the devil who has tried to destroy your family, then you can pull down and come against what was meant to destroy you!

How Do You Know When You Have Forgiven Someone?

Once upon a time, I saw two different movies about the same thing. The first movie was a story about a young man who was abused throughout his life. He was taken advantage of in a foster home setting. In this story, he went back years later to confront his abusers. The other movie was about a young girl who was growing up in the south and forced to marry someone and become his slave. She didn't even know his real name because she was his cook and cleaning lady. At the end of her story, she confronted her abuser as well.

Both movies had characters who did the same thing. They told their abusers that they were not going to become what they tried to do to them. They told their abusers that they had survived the abuse and were not going to be stuck in what they tried to do to them.

When you can look people in the eye, whom the devil has used to do evil against you and understand that they didn't know any better, you know you have forgiven. All they did was set you up to find Jesus! Even though they let the devil use them to hurt you, they really hurt themselves in the process and not you. Why? Because you are still here!

No weapon that is formed against thee shall prosper; and every tongue that shall rise against thee in judgment thou shalt condemn. This is the heritage of the servants of the LORD, and their righteousness is of me, saith the LORD.

(Isaiah 54:17, KJV)

Are you ready to be healed? Are you ready to forgive yourself for what you've done and forgive others for what has been done unto you? How do I know that I've gotten my focus off people and back on God's destiny for my life to become whole?

First, get your focus off yourself and onto God. The woman with the issue of blood focused upon who Jesus was and not who she was. In order to get past what you've done and what was done unto you, it's time to focus upon Jesus. "When she had heard of Jesus, came in the press behind..." (Mark 5:27, KJV). She heard of Jesus and what He could do for her, and that was enough. She heard that He could heal blinded eyes, resurrect the dead, and lay hands on the sick. When she began to focus upon Jesus, her faith became provoked in order to become healed.

It's time to stop looking at your problem and blaming yourself and others for why you are in this thing and begin to magnify and worship God.

Remember:

- He is Lord of all, even for your situation that seems out of control!
- He is the Prince of peace for your distressing situation!
- He is the bright and morning star for your dark situation!
- He is the everlasting God for your long-lasting situation!

Second, you need to press your way to God and give it all you've got to become whole. Join a gym, church, social group, Bible study, or whatever it takes to move into the healing phase of your life and away from being a victim of whatever was done to you that's made you unforgiving. The woman in this passage applies an enormous amount of physical and spiritual strength to extend herself to reach Jesus.

What are you doing to go beyond yourself in order to become healed and whole in this area of your life? Some of us place all the emphasis upon Jesus and forget that we have a part to play in this too. She put herself in a position to be healed when she pressed her way to Jesus. "When she had heard of Jesus, came in the press behind, and touched his garment" (Mark 5:27, KJV). "Press" in this passage is better translated as the *"extension of people"* because that's what a press is, an extension of yourself. Whenever you press, you extend beyond yourself:

Remember:

- You extend beyond your natural ability!
- You extend beyond your own strength and power!
- You extend beyond yourself!

Brethren, I count not myself to have apprehended: but this one thing I do, forgetting those things which are behind, and reaching forth unto those things which are before, I press toward the mark for the prize of the high calling of God in Christ Jesus.

(Philippians 3:13–14, KJV)

We have to do whatever it takes to press towards wholeness in life. It is easier to give up whenever it comes down to doing something we really don't want to do. For example, if you don't want to clean your house, then you will make excuses for why you live in a mess. Your clothes will not get washed or hung up. Your kitchen will maintain a sink full of dishes, and you will make excuse after excuse for why you aren't cleaning. Just the same, do not stop short of wholeness by not forgiving others and yourself. Do whatever it takes to dislodge people from your heart and mind.

Finally, you actually have to believe that God can make you whole again. Do you have a vision of your freed-up self? Can you see yourself living better than this? This woman believed that Jesus would heal her, so she believed. "For she said, 'If I may touch but his clothes, I shall be whole" (Mark 5:28, KJV). She did her part and left the rest up to God.

Questions:

- Do you really believe that God can heal you of a broken heart?
- Do you really believe that God can take away a nasty attitude?
- Do you really believe that God can break a bad habit for you?

- Do you really believe that you can forgive others and yourself?

If so, then cry out to God and ask Him to help you moment by moment to release yourself and others. When this woman in the Bible reached out to Jesus, something happened. "And straightway the fountain of her blood was dried up; and she felt in her body that she was healed of that plague" (Mark 5:29, KJV). At the end of the story, Jesus states, "And he said unto her, 'Daughter, thy faith hath made thee whole; go in peace, and be whole of thy plague'" (Mark 5:34, KJV).

To be freed-up from unforgiveness moves you out of hurt and into healing so that you may reach your destiny. Ultimately, how bad do you desire wholeness in your life?

2.

Moving Out of Your Way
I Forgive Myself!

John 4:11-14

God has a way of bringing lessons to us that become our opportunities to grow and change. These are situations that teach us about His lordship and our humanity until we crave His presence and transformation through Him. If you're going to become a whole person and enjoy your life, then you have to see that nothing is an accident. God sets up life as a classroom to teach us about who He is and who we are in Christ. You can almost miss the lessons that God has for you and how pregnant you are with God's promises by focusing upon the wrong things. In fact, it doesn't always have to be something negative that is teaching you something positive in life. Sometimes, there can be something negative teaching you something positive about yourself. If you aren't an open person, then you will miss what is right in front of you as a lesson for your new season of change. Because life is exploratory, discovery-based, and adventurous, there are some things you will learn as you go out into the world and experience them for yourselves. Additionally, there are lessons that God brings right to wherever you are because otherwise, you would miss it.

When I was in seminary, Dr. Tony Evans of the Urban Alternative and pastor of Oak Cliff Bible Fellowship in Dallas, Texas, came to speak at my school. Dr. Evans is known for his riveting books, expository teaching, and affiliations as the chaplain of the Dallas Cowboys (NFL) and Dallas Mavericks (NBA). When the campus pastor's office called me while I was a freshman seminary student and asked if I would be available to pick him up from the airport, take him to his speaking engagement on campus, drop him off to his lunch appointment, bring him to the hotel to freshen up, and then circle back to take him to the airport later on that night, I almost fell off my chair! To have exclusive time with Dr. Evans and drive him around in my two-door Chevy Cavalier was an amazing experience in my life. I couldn't believe that I was driving around Dr. Evans and asking him questions from leadership to courtship to marriage. At that time, I wasn't married to my college sweetheart yet, and Dr. Evans's advice was so simplistic and timely.

I also knew that I had heard him give this same advice on the radio, television, and in one of his many books, but now it was targeted to me in a more personal conversation. God sent Dr. Evans to me to talk about my purpose, plan, and God's provision. At that point in my life, I had never traveled to Dallas, Texas, to see him in person, yet God brought a preacher from Dallas to me to change my life forever. Just the same, God meets us where we are to bring His lessons of forgiveness to us so that we may move on with our lives!

The story of a woman who meets Jesus at the well is one also of God's divine appointments. This woman, being a Samaritan, would have never been able to come to Jesus nor seek Him out, but she somehow winds up at the well. After spending time with this man who actually was the Son of God, her life was changed forever. She had an appointment with forgiveness that she wasn't even aware of, and Jesus coming to her was in the plan of God.

Why did Jesus come to her? John, the theologian, records the events and activities of Jesus' growing popularity, the Bible states, "Now Jesus learned that the Pharisees had heard that he was gaining and baptizing more disciples than John" (John 4:1, NIV). The pharisees, the religious and devout followers of the law, were ready to confront Jesus. They wanted to talk to Jesus about who He thought He was because they did not believe He was the Son of God, although He performed miracles and teachings with the power of God.

Therefore, Jesus, who is not ready to reveal His ultimate plans, leaves the city of Judea according to John 4:2, and heads to the city of Galilee. When Jesus left the city, John, the author, shares and prepares our hearts to read about Jesus' redirections. God doesn't change the plan, He changes the man! Jesus in His human-like qualities as He lived on this earth, shows us that God's direction involves His protection. Jesus detoured, not for preservation purposes, but because God had another plan for Him to pass through where this woman was.

Are You Walking in the Plan of Man or in the Protection of God's Direction?

Jesus decided to leave for His own reasons. To get from Judea to Galilee, He chose an unpopular route to travel. Jesus, being a Jew, wouldn't normally journey through the city of Samaria because most Jews couldn't stand the Samaritan people. They would rather walk around the city of Samaria and take several extra days out of their journey to get to their destination. But, according to John 4:4, Jesus needed to go through Samaria because God had a purpose for Him in that place.

Before you make a change, such as a new job, house, church, and/or walk away from a good man or woman, can you still see that God always has a purpose for you in the new place? Likewise, God had an appointment for Jesus and this Samaritan woman right in the most unpopular place for a Jew to travel. Nevertheless, in order to know your purpose, you have to move past your feelings, emotions, and disappointments until you see God's appointment in a certain place. Sometimes, it's not the place you're in that needs to change... it's you, the person in the place, who may need to change!

Therefore, here is Jesus walking to Galilee, a place He calls home. To get there, He goes through Sychar, a city a few miles southeast of Samaria. He approaches a woman at a well, and both the woman and the well are very similar.

The well was given to Jacob some hundred years before, and in Genesis 33:19, it served a purpose. Just the same, this non-Jewish woman had been living her life in relationships with numerous men. For God and us today, she serves a purpose. She helps us to see that life is full of God's divine appointments.

In John 4:7–9, Jesus says to this woman that she is worth something to God because God doesn't assign our value to us based upon where we live or how much money we have. No, we've been made in the image of God! To the Jews, Samaritans were considered dogs and less than human, but Jesus explains to her that she is worth spending time with.

Sadly, too many people in the world receive their worth from other people, their clothing, and how their hair and nails are done. The reality is that our worth comes from being made in the image of God.

Remember:

- You are beautiful to God!
- You are special to Him!
- You are precious in His sight!

"I will praise thee; for I am fearfully and wonderfully made: marvelous are thy works; and that my soul knoweth right well" (Psalm 139:14, KJV). Sometimes, how we let people treat us is an indication of how we see our value. Some of us think too lowly of ourselves rather than seeing the worth we have been given from God. For this reason, it is oftentimes difficult to become healed and a whole person because there's a lie telling you that you somehow deserve to be treated negatively! No matter how appointed you are by God, you need to understand something... If you do not believe in how unique and special you are to God, then you can become overwhelmed with disappointment because you will somehow think that the world gets to dictate happiness and joy to you!

In order to move on with your life into forgiveness, you have to deal with your disappointments. Why are you struggling with unforgiveness in the first place? What happened to you that you've become bitter and not better? In fact, if you don't deal with your unforgiving heart, you will become a person who has been typecasted by one negative experience that now has defined your life. One unchecked disappointment can lead to a lifetime of unhappiness.

In John 4:10–14, this woman deals with two major disappointments, although she is at the well with Jesus.

First, a major disappointment for her is her physical inability to draw water. This well is about one hundred feet deep into the ground. The woman says that she doesn't have a rope and a bucket that will go down into the ground and pull up water for Jesus. However, Jesus was not asking her about physical water! Jesus was addressing her inner, spiritual problem. Do not think for a moment that God cannot see your inner problem of unforgivingness. We try to hide and dress it up, but God sees right into our lives and unearths the hidden pains of holding grudges, burrowing anger, and pretending like our disappointments don't exist.

Second, her disappointment was her spiritual insecurity about life. This woman was unsure of who she was in life, and therefore, her larger inabilities were also spiritually related. There are so many of us living an unsatisfied life that is blocked by the unforgiveness in our hearts. Nothing causes us to become blind from our glorious outlook, seeing the sunrise every day with excitement, and living through year after year like unforgiveness. Be careful whenever you allow your past to define you; you are more than a total of your experiences and cannot be defined by whatever has happened to you.

Declaration: *I am not whatever has happened to me; it happened to me, but I am not it!*

In John 4:16–18, Jesus goes right to the heart of the matter and confronts her real problem—she needs to forgive herself. Notice something about this woman. For all intents and purposes, she does not want to talk about her past. In fact, in the next several verses of John 4:19–24, she changes the subject and avoids the topic Jesus brings up.

A lot of times, whenever we are dealing with our ashamed past, it's usually because of something someone else has done to us. We complain about others and what they've done and find it hard to get past it. Additionally, we fight over silly things that people have done to us, but we're not dealing with the real problem. Have you ever been given so much grief by a person that you thought, *There's no way I could be your problem!* For most of us, we would rather ignore how we're treating the other person and focus on how the other person is treating us. When you realize that you're the problem, it hurts too much.

Some people blame everyone and everything around them except for themselves because it's easier to blame others rather than deal with whatever they've done personally. Jesus was dealing with this woman's mistakes in her past relationships, but she shifts the conversation to where the Jews claimed they should worship. If you're going to forgive others and keep it moving, then you must begin with being able to forgive yourself.

When I first got married to my wife, I raked the leaves in our new backyard into a pile and then didn't know what to do with them. We were living in a new area, and I had no idea how the county collected leaves or expected residents to dispose of them. Fortunately, all of a sudden, I remembered the smell of burning leaves, and the idea came to me while my wife was inside preparing dinner. It seemed like a great idea at first. After all, I was in my early twenties and still learning how to become a homeowner. Unlike the first year of our marriage when we lived in an apartment, I now had these leaves to account for. So, I gathered the leaves into a humongous pile and thought, *I need an accelerant* to burn the leaves. Now, what you read here is about one of the dumbest things I've ever done in my life!

Scientists and medical doctors tell us that the

frontal lobe of the brain is not fully developed in our early twenties. For this reason, our sense of judgment or common sense can be a little bit off. My point is that I used gasoline to burn the leaves. Let's just say I never got the match close enough to the pile of leaves to burn them. After I wet the leaves with gas and began to approach the pile, there was an explosion in the air that threw me on my back about ten feet from the leaf pile. The explosive sound was loud, and I saw red and orange crackles in the sky as I laid on my back looking upward. Immediately, I felt for my eyebrows for some reason, and thankfully, they were still there. At this point in my life, this was the dumbest thing I had ever done, and with great embarrassment, I now needed to forgive myself.

My wife asked me later that evening if I heard the booming sound earlier. My answer at that time was laced with embarrassment. I asked her, *"What sound?"* Of course, I almost blew up the backyard using gasoline to burn the leaves, but at that moment, I didn't want to talk about my foolish decision and almost fatal consequences. At that moment, I had to explain to her what happened. Like the woman at the well, no one wants to talk about the dumb things they've done!

However, the real things that we find hard to forgive ourselves for doing, no one ever really knows the complete details. It's easier to disappear from people and say nothing when we exit. This is one thing that we say: *"Lord, if you ever get me out of this, then I will become a church usher or some-*

thing!" We do not tell anyone about the things we've all done that we are ashamed of, yet the devil reminds us of our mistakes over and over again. Revelation 12:10 (KJV) calls Satan the "accuser of our brethren" because the devil keeps reminding us of what we've done.

What Are You Hiding That's Making It Difficult to Forgive Yourself and Move On? Whenever the devil tries to get you to replay what you've done in the past over and over again, it's to rob you of your future. The devil is trying to get you to make a connection between what you've done and who you are, but they are not the same thing. The devil wants you to be stuck in a life that's forever looking back on what you've done. He also wants you to always introduce yourself to others according to what you've done, so they will know how to treat you. Whenever you send out a signal of abuse, people who mean you harm will exploit this about you. When this happens, you'll spend the next forty years trying to convince people and God that you are a good person. Remember, here is the Son of God standing next to the woman at the well, yet she doesn't even get it because the devil has a way of trying to blind us from receiving God's forgiveness.

Have you ever been reminded of what you've done? Have you ever kept seeing over and over again what you've done? The devil would love to manipulate your mind by causing you to think that God has somehow not forgiven you of what you've done. Like you, most of my mistakes stay on my mind. At times, I can still see where I was, and when I did what I did.

Later comes the thoughts of guilt about how I knew I was wrong when I did it. I can still hear what I heard when I did what I did and how I heard this voice in my ear saying I was wrong for what I did when I did it. The devil wants to convince you that you are not forgiven so that you will stay stuck in the past. Too many times, as you and I have found, it is hard to shake our past. Whenever we cannot shake what we've done, it will try to kill you.

In John, chapter 4, this woman at the well knew she had five husbands and a new man currently in her house that wasn't her husband. She knew her mistakes and how she couldn't shake the agony of whatever she had done. As she stood there with the Son of God, she knew this man could see right into her soul. She immediately realized that, at that moment, she didn't like herself. I have tried to help all kinds of people in my life, but the hardest ones to reach are the ones who don't like themselves.

What Do You Do When You Don't Even like Yourself?

If you are not careful, then you will begin to think that God has not forgiven you. Even some of you could admit that you think God is still angry with you. What keeps many of us in a cycle of sin is not being able to shake **this feeling**, so you think, *I might as well keep on sinning because whether I commit this sin or I am living right, I still feel the same way!*

Could it be that some of us are asleep to the fact that God has forgiven us for whatever we've ever done, and now you need to forgive yourself? God has forgiven you, yet it may not feel like it. Actually, the devil doesn't want you to believe God has forgiven you. He wants you to think God is still angry with you. Today, some of you are going to miss your intimacy with God because of what the devil is telling you. The devil was telling this woman that she was being judged for who she was and what she did. Even more, this woman was judged for her race and then for her mistakes! For some people, they would say, *"Who does she think she is talking to Jesus?"*

Have you ever been praying or in church and the devil whispers to you something similar? Some people hear the devil speaking and think it's the church or the pastor, but in fact, it's coming from below the earth. Moreover, they hear the enemy say, *"Get out, get out, and leave!"*

I'm sure this woman was tempted at some point to stop talking to Jesus. Some of you have been living right, but because of what the devil has said about you, you've been tempted to stop living right too. Unforgiveness of ourselves holds us all down as prisoners of our past and locked into whatever we've done.

> Let us therefore come boldly unto the throne of grace, that we may obtain mercy, and find grace to help in time of need.
>
> (Hebrews 4:16, KJV)

Remember:

- It doesn't matter what you've done.
- It doesn't matter how you have failed God.
- It doesn't matter what you keep coming back to.

You've got God's amazing grace. Grace that is greater than all your and my sins. The devil tries to create distance between you and people, so you don't reach an intimate place with God. This even happens with our relationship with God. Too many people let the devil stop them from giving their life to Him. Too many Christians let the devil stop them from attending church. Too many Christians let the devil stop them from joining or serving in a church. Don't let the devil stop you from being intimate with God. However, we don't have time to be at odds with God or people by harboring things against ourselves. You don't have time to allow arguments and disappointments within yourself to keep you from God. All you have to do is realize who Jesus is.

How do I snap out of all of this? This woman probably thought to herself, *Wait a minute, Jesus wants to talk to me and give me water, so I would never thirst again?* She told Jesus earlier that she didn't have anything to fetch water with, but she had a water pot! Undoubtedly, she didn't come to draw her own water but was hoping someone else would have a rope and a bucket to fetch her some water. In actuality, she came to the well to receive relief from the Son of God. In regard to the water pot and what it represents, it is her receiving eternal water and relief from the heaviness of unforgiveness. It's time to forgive, live, and let go of your water pot.

3.

Moving into Action

The Commitment to Forgiveness

Luke 7:38-50

A lot of us want the dividends of forgiveness without the work. Whenever we fail to put the work in, we should not expect the reward. There are so many Christians today who want God to do all the work of placing forgiveness in their hearts. However, they forget that there's an expected input that is required from them. For example, it is possible that you are reading this book and thinking that God is going to give you a heart of forgiveness. In reality, God and you need to work it out together for you to develop a heart of forgiveness.

We all want a miracle pill that we can take whenever we have had too many honey buns or too much ice cream. We want a miracle pill that allows us to eat whatever we want and automatically melt away our fat and the numerous calories in our body caused by our constant diet of junk food. While this may sound silly, you can be hooked on unforgiveness like a person who believes that all the ownness for your spiritual freedom and moving on is God's job and not yours.

Never become a person who doesn't work and expects everyone to give them something. If you don't put the work in for forgiveness, then it doesn't just happen for you. Stop asking God for miracle pills to melt your unforgiving heart. Just put the work in!

Oftentimes, we are committed to our own asking and receiving what we need from God rather than giving what is needed and obeying Him. A non-committed person is like someone who wants to become a doctor but doesn't want to go to medical school. We have to give God something to work with in order to see the living fruit of our commitment in an idea, craft, talent, concept, desire, goal, and/or destiny.

Our commitment to walking in forgiveness must be both enabled by God and self-motivation. As long as we want God to invade our thinking and remove unforgiveness, we will fail to see our part in it. Your commitment to walk in your destiny and rid yourself of the pain of unforgiveness is up to you. We are living in a time of putting minimal effort into things and expecting big results. You can't "sleep in" through life and expect God to just hand you things without you going to work. God is our good Father and will take care of us, but never think that He intends for you to be a baby bird in the nest all your life. We have to arrest the notion that the heavy lifting is all on God instead of there being a joint effort and partnership with Him to usher blessings into our lives through self-pruning and productivity. Forgiveness is a choice, and breaking the spirit of unforgiveness is a commitment.

Remember Jesus' visit to a house full of pharisees? If He came to these stout, religious leaders' homes, then certainly He will visit wherever you are! In Luke, chapter 7, Jesus went to an unlikely place and while at this house, there were two incredible examples of a commitment to wholeness and moving on.

First, we see the tenacity of our savior. Jesus came to where these people were when He visited a place where no one would have expected Him. Do you know that Jesus' love is available in the toughest cities? Moreover, God's presence is in the homeless shelter? The Holy Spirit dwells in broken places, and we should never think that God cannot meet us where we are!

Whenever you think about God delivering you from the spirit of unforgiveness, you have to understand that God does things that seem out of place to others. Yes, He will meet you wherever you are! It doesn't even matter if you've cursed the day your antagonist, enemies, and/or haters were born, God will meet you wherever you are and help you to forgive them. While work is still required on your part, don't think that God will somehow skip you because of how low you've thought of someone or how hard it's been to forgive them. God loves us despite our mistakes, and He will meet you wherever you are.

Do you see God in the midst of your unforgiving situation? Believe it because He is there!

You may be dealing with pain caused by someone and have been going back and forth about letting them go, but God will help you to forgive someone if you're willing to put in the work. Jesus demonstrates that God is not partial. He goes into unpopular places or meets the least likable people to remind us of God's grace towards us all.

In Luke 7:36, Jesus had come to a pharisee's house to have a meal with him. The pharisees were a band of devout Jewish religious leaders who were more recognized by their holiness on the outside, including their clothing and the words they spoke, than their holiness on the inside in which the condition of their hearts were not right. Followers of Jesus, and even the world at that time didn't have great respect for the pharisees because of their hypocrisy. However, Jesus still took the time to go past this pharisee's house and have dinner with him. This was an odd act of Jesus to come into this man's house because it was different for Jesus to have been seen in this man's house for dinner. For all intents and purposes, Jesus even seemed out of place to everyone.

God will show up for your situation!

Do you remember the original movie, *Guess Who's Coming to Dinner,* starring Sidney Poitier, Katherine Hepburn, and Spencer Tracey? This is a story about a young, fair lady who brings home Sidney Poitier for dinner to meet her family. Everyone was surprised to find out that he was black. The common reaction in this movie was, "What is he doing in here?" Likewise, this same sort of attitude from others was demonstrated when Jesus entered into this man's house. The common reaction by His disciples was probably, "What are you doing in here, Jesus?"

Even though there was resistance to His actions, Jesus still took the time to come by this man's house. Despite how foul and pollutant this man really was, Jesus still came to his house and met with him. Therefore, Jesus will come down to wherever you are and meet you, too.

Wherever you are on the road to forgiveness, God will meet with you and never turn you away. It doesn't matter how badly you've thought of someone who hurt you, God is loving and will forgive all of us. Psalm 139 reminds us of the inescapability of God and how He is everywhere we go. You could be reading this book from a prison cell or while sitting on your porch sipping ice tea. Regardless of where you are, God is right there with you!

Don't excommunicate God by your circumstance and think that He can't somehow reach you. God is an equal opportunity God, and He will meet you wherever you are. It is possible that you are reading this book with tears or even God forbid, you're ready to commit to ending your pain the wrong way by hurting others or yourself. Today, look up and understand that God has not somehow forgotten you because He's right where you are! God is committed to reaching you!

The second example of commitment we see is also in Luke, chapter 7, when a woman who wasn't well-respected showed up at the same house and anointed Jesus' feet. She was committed to getting her own personal, spiritual healing and encounter with Jesus.

Luke, chapter 7, also introduces to us a woman who sat at Jesus' feet. "And, behold, a woman in the city, which was a sinner, when she knew that Jesus sat at meat in the pharisee's house, brought an alabaster box of ointment" (Luke 7:37, KJV). Undoubtedly, this woman was now being judged for her involvement at the pharisee's house. It was a social risk for Jesus to come to the pharisee's house to begin with, but an even bigger risk for this woman to show up at the pharisee's house to see Jesus.

In fact, Luke 7:39 calls this woman a "sinner". What keeps us locked up in any sin, weight, or condition is when we let people reduce others from being a child of God to whatever we've done in our past as our new name. Nevertheless, whenever you get ready to forgive someone, you're reminded of your mistakes, and the pain you've incurred that has now type casted you by your past mistakes. The enemy wants you to focus on you being the victim and not to worry about forgiveness. However, from the example of this woman who comes to see Jesus, we see that you can't allow your circumstances to rob you from God's blessings for your life.

Never allow your past mistakes and hurts to keep you from making it to the presence of God and making a commitment to being healed from unforgiveness! This woman doesn't know the right things to say to Jesus. She doesn't really know how to even worship Jesus or how to interact with Him in spiritual conversations. Furthermore, she doesn't even know how to carry herself around Jesus or know all of the Scriptures. She is just someone who got tired of carrying around her pain and wanted to be in the presence of Jesus.

How bad do you want it?

...A broken and a contrite heart, O God, thou wilt not despise.

(Psalm 51:17, KJV)

If you are not careful, then you can despise yourself to the place where you will not allow God to bless you with something as simple as a joyous heart, a peaceful mind, or a spirit of forgiveness. There is a part of us that feels undeserving of God's best, which causes us to miss what He has for us. That will lead us to spend the next forty years of our lives trying to convince God that we are good people. The pharisee received the gift of Jesus' presence in his house, but this woman goes after the gift of forgiveness and fights through the feeling of inadequacy to receive God's forgiveness.

Whenever you keep reminding yourself of whatever you've done or what was done to you, you will stop short in walking in forgiveness. If you are not careful, then you will begin to think that God has not forgiven you. Come on, some of you have to admit you think God is still angry with you. Because you think your mother or father is still angry with you, this keeps many of us in a cycle of not forgiving others and not being able to shake this feeling. As long as you find it hard to forgive yourself or believe

43

that God and others haven't forgiven you of something, it makes it easier for you to hold on to unforgiveness.

While this woman was anointing Jesus' feet, she had to both forgive herself and those who were jeering in the background as they judged her while she came to Jesus to be forgiven. There was a commitment involved on this woman's part to forgive as she was also being forgiven. Usually, everything is fine until the accuser comes. Some of you were doing all right in different situations until you heard what your family, friends, or even strangers said around you. Ultimately, this woman had forgiven others while being forgiven by God!

I don't know about you, but there are too many things that I've let people talk me out of. There have been too many desires that I have turned my back on because of other people. One of the biggest things you should never do is surrender to the enemy. You have the right to come into the presence of God.

> Let us therefore come boldly unto the throne of grace, that we may obtain mercy, and find grace to help in time of need.

> (Hebrew 4:16, KJV)

It doesn't matter what you've done and how you may have failed others and yourself; God's grace is greater! This woman was on her hands and knees worshipping Jesus and receiving the forgiveness of God while she heard the jeers and sneers from the people nearby. I'm sure she wanted to stop worshipping Jesus and break her commitment to having a heart of forgiveness, but she didn't. The moment you decide to change or do better, something will always want to challenge your commitment. In order for you to get to a place of intimacy with God, you are going to have to press against whatever you've done and whatever people say and stay committed.

When you really want a breakthrough in your life, your commitment will scare others. For example, the pharisees could not understand this woman's level of intensity. "And stood at his feet behind him weeping, and began to wash his feet with tears, and did wipe them with the hairs of her head, and kissed his feet, and anointed them with the ointment" (Luke 7:38, KJV). When you really want to have a heart of forgiveness, you will read books, study, pray, fast, highlight your Bible with a yellow marker, and attend conferences, among many other things. You will call those who may have mistreated or abused you and meet them for lunch or even remove yourself from their presence to be made whole.

How bad do you want your breakthrough? The fact that she poured out a bottle of oil on Jesus' feet to wash them with her tears, hair, and then get on her hands and knees at His feet showed that she had a different level of intensity than those who judged her. All she had to do was accept God's forgiveness towards her, which she did. For this reason, she could forgive others around her. This woman showed us that she made a firm commitment to getting what she wanted from Jesus and giving what she wanted to Jesus, which was to pour oil in worship to Him.

There will be people who will not understand the level of your sacrifice in order to walk in the freedom of forgiveness. The people around her could not understand the level of her sacrifice because they didn't know the price of her alabaster box. They didn't know that she had to overcome her past to worship God. See, nothing helps us to walk in forgiveness like worship. Whenever we focus upon what God does and who He is, it helps us to overcome what people have done and who we are.

In fact, in Luke 7:44–47, the disciples and pharisees questioned this woman being able to touch Jesus. But He pointed out how no one was as hospitable to Him as she was in the pharisee's house. Jesus said that because this woman had great sin, she also had great worship.

Have you had terrible things done to you? Have you received horrid actions against you? Have you experienced the worst in life? Have you admittingly done wrong to others? If so, your worship should be great! In other words, because God had forgiven this woman of so much, she couldn't stop worshipping Him. We should be the same way.

How do we worship God then? Worship is not just a song or a prayer. Worship is when we embrace the presence of God and become transformed in His presence. In Luke 7:38, this woman demonstrates how she wanted to worship Jesus. When you truly embrace how much God loves and forgives you, it will do more than make you cry and lift your hands. Real worship is a lifestyle of honor and glory to God.

Once you understand this, you can forgive others whenever you realize how much God has forgiven you.

Luke 12:48 is about being given much by God. Therefore, He can require much from us as well. Whenever you think about how much God has forgiven you, let it take you to a place of worshipping Him with your life and walking in His forgiveness towards others.

> And he said to the woman, Thy faith hath saved thee; go in peace.
>
> (Luke 7:50, KJV)

This idea of peace is emphasized in this passage because it was meant for us to understand that forgiveness is something you both give and receive. Because God has forgiven you, you have peace with God. Therefore, this step in walking in forgiveness includes accepting God's forgiveness.

Whenever you're on an airplane, there's a series of pre-flight announcements from the flight crew. One of the announcements has to do with the plane possibly losing cabin pressure and how to access your overhead oxygen mask. We're told that if the plane loses cabin pressure, an oxygen mask will descend from an overhead compartment. If we're seated next to a small child, we must first place the mask on ourselves and then put the mask on the small child beside us. Before you try to forgive someone, receive the forgiveness of God first.

Make a commitment to receiving God's forgiveness at hand and then offer it to others.

Ask yourself:

- Am I committed to being forgiven?
- Am I committed to forgiving others?
- Am I committed to being in the presence of God?

4.

Moving Back into Play

Bouncing Back

1 Peter 4:12-14

It was a cold winter afternoon. As the students were running on the playground, they could see their breath. Unfortunately, there was a small gathering of sibling girls who were without coats amongst the students, and they stood shivering and huddled together not too far from the teachers who were on recess duty. Even though these girls didn't have coats, they were required to join the rest of the class outside, no matter the temperature. They noticed warm vapor, which looked like heavy steam floating in the air, coming from the grates on the city streets. Unfortunately, the grates were located outside the gates of the school, where recess was taking place and seemed like miles away from these shivering girls. This experience was a typical moment for these girls and a regular experience for my mother, who huddled with her sisters on the playground to keep warm, too.

When my mother was growing up, she attended eleven elementary schools. It became apparent to her early in life that even though her parents loved her, she was going to have to fight to overcome the odds of poverty, lack of opportunities, and a life of consequences due to the adults in her life. Simple toiletries and a warm coat to wear outside were little necessities that often bypassed her as a child. Growing up in a single-parent home, her mom and sisters often lived with other people. This is not typically the best recipe for developing big dreams.

My mother dreamed of things like making it through the night, getting her next meal, and being able to get her schoolwork finished amidst a heap of distractions. It seemed almost unfair that her childhood play and imagination were interrupted by having to survive life in the inner city. My mother eventually devoted her life to Christ and helping others. Specifically, she believed in women encouraging each other, and for this reason, she was the founder of *Sisters Keepers International* and a conglomerate group of women called *Uniting Sisters*. She has helped thousands of women because she was able to move beyond her early struggles in life by having a heart of forgiveness.

My mother doesn't have the stench of her experiences on her because she has forgiven others and moved on. She has ministered to thousands of women by moving on and bouncing back. When you realize that your life has been a set up for greatness and not failure, then like my mother, you will see your opposition as an opportunity to help others to move on from unforgiveness. No matter how difficult it has become for you, you can actually do this and make an impact in the lives of others.

Can you imagine that a person who was so hurt by life is now being used to heal the lives of others? My mother sold Avon and became an Avon district manager because she was good at connecting with people. It wasn't about the product; it was about her investment in people. She had an excuse to work with women who became top sales producers in their areas through her management and guidance because it was bigger than soaps and lotions. Not only was she glad to be able to see others with great cosmetics and toiletries through Avon, but she was blessed to be able to have a vehicle to reach out to many women across the metropolitan area.

Her bouncing back from her rough childhood was in connecting with many women who, like herself, needed encouragement. To hear from someone that the negative moments of their lives were somehow in the plan of God as a means of drawing him or her closer to Him and not further away makes the suffering worth it. What is God using in your life that is not meant for your demise, but somehow for your promotion to be the bridge that crosses you over into forgiveness and helping to heal others?

My father was a young man growing up in the South. He lived with his parents and ten other siblings, which is a lot of mouths to feed. With eleven growing children, growing up in the country needed more than the essentials. His family loved each other, and getting by during the 1940s and 1950s was not easy in the South, especially when there was no indoor plumbing.

The social rules during segregation took a much heavier toll on kids who lived in areas where federal laws ending segregation were ignored, and local laws carried on as usual, with many refusing to change with the times. It was even harder for kids whose homes were dismantled by poverty, absent parents, abuse, and adults dealing with addictions. My father didn't fit into all of these categories, but after losing both parents, older siblings were left to fill in the shoes of his deceased parents.

I think my father saw things in his past that he would love to forget. Furthermore, to lose a sibling who was the closest to his age at that time was devastating. A freakish accident involving his brother left him without his closest friend in a blink of an eye. If it weren't for the Lord and organized sports, my father would have lost his mind. His start in the world seemed challenged from day one because of where he lived and how he grew up, but it was also the thing that he used to bounce back in life.

Most of the Generation Xers wouldn't be able to survive that time period because we came along during a time of great spending and credit in this country. Our priorities became skewed as television began to glamorize materialism, and the invention of music videos was a way of communicating to us what every teenager should have. I think my father was glad to have his brother's hand-me-downs, something simple to eat or drink, and a warm bed to sleep on at night. The idea of an Atari Gaming System, Sony Walkman, an electric football set, and a new bicycle were foreign to him.

Because my father devoted so much of his time and attention to playing sports, he lettered in five sports in high school. When I was a small child, my father would brag to his friends that he once won games against devoted golfers with one club for every hole. He moved from the poor South to a poor city, but he brought his resilience with him from the country.

As children, my siblings and I watched our father play basketball and football from the stands and play baseball in parks, gyms, and recreation centers until he became too old to play. When my father stopped playing, he started coaching.

My father became one of the winningest basketball and baseball coaches in the city. He taught his players, including my siblings and me, the value of hard work and to make sure that you put 100% in every game and practice. Additionally, my father applied his work ethics to helping others. As children, we fed the homeless, supported street evangelism efforts, and visited nursing homes and hospitals with him to promote humanity and give people hope in God. My father got trounced by life but bounced back with a heart of forgiveness.

If you've been knocked down by life, then keep reading this chapter!

This chapter is really devoted to those of you who got knocked down in life by others and now find it hard to get up and bounce back. There's a passage I love in the Bible that speaks to the suddenly that trials bring and how the Apostle Peter spoke to those who are caught off guard by trouble.

1 Peter 4:12–14 is about a church that was surviving persecution. This church needed to forgive others and then bounce back. This passage reveals that we are to do the same as Christians who underwent suffering and the exhortation to prayer, hospitality, and Christian character during times of trouble caused by others. The apostle makes it clear that we are to remain blameless during the most difficult times of suffering with the help of Christ as our example and the Holy Spirit as our enabler and providing such sufficiency.

Peter is one of three apostles and disciples of Jesus, the others being Matthew and John, to write a New Testament Book. Peter's name appears some 210 times in the New Testament, whereas the names of the other eleven apostles appear only 142 times in total. Therefore, Peter is a significant author to us because he was a significant apostle to Christ. Around 64 AD, Peter writes this epistle we're reading on the eve of an outbreak of persecution against the Christians:

Nero, the Roman emperor who ascended to the throne after the death of his Great-Uncle Claudius in 54 AD, was killing Christians. He was the replacement of his uncle/emperor Claudius, who replaced emperor Caligula. As each Roman ruler replaced another one, each one became worse. Each emperor's persecution brought more diabolical and horrific persecution for God's people. One even had the nerve to order the killing of Jesus at the hand of the Jewish leaders.

Can you imagine living during this time period? Each leader was more evil than the prior, and each situation made the conditions for the Jews more horrid. Nevertheless, each time a new emperor was chosen, the people prayed that the new one would be better than their predecessor. Instead, the situation became worse.

One of the hardest times to forgive is when people in our lives make our bad situations worse. If you are already down and someone comes along and gives you a hard time, it makes it even harder to forgive them. I mean, if I'm lying on the ground and you come along and kick me, then it's even more disappointing. Sometimes we are surrounded by people who have fallen down in life, and our interaction makes them feel like they were kicked. These types of situations make it even harder to forgive when you're already doing bad.

I remember my step-grandfather taking my brother and me with him to the corner store when I was a kid. We were visiting my grandmother in the city and going to the store with him was not a regular thing. We would always walk past people hanging out in a park partaking on beverages wrapped in brown paper bags. I had no concept of what they were doing, although, in my nine-year-old conscience, I could tell something wasn't right. My grandfather had a tall, thin stature and stood above my small, potbelly frame. As I walked closely beside him, we came upon these suspect-looking individuals in the park. As we got closer, there was a pigeon with a broken wing on the ground walking around.

A few of the men had the bird cornered and began to throw rocks.

My grandfather was very upset, yet with a tear in his eye, he walked past the men throwing rocks at the bird and said nothing. I remember asking him why he didn't say something to the men about the helpless bird. My grandfather told me he knew that the bird was already going to die because of its broken wing. However, in his heart, I could tell he wanted to demand mercy for the bird that was slowly dying.

Are You like a Bird with a Broken Wing? Whenever we have a broken wing and others come along and throw rocks, it only makes it worse. God wants to heal the broken wings of every individual. However, it is hard to heal when others come along and hurt us while we are already hurting. Have you ever been kicked while you were already down? It's hard to get up when you feel like someone keeps putting you down. However, you can bounce back from this.

The bird reminded me of the woman who was brought to Jesus because of her sin, and the pharisees were ready to stone her. When Jesus was asked if her punishment of stoning was appropriate, He replied that only those who had no sin should throw rocks. I guess this woman also felt bad because of her sin and stoning her would have also made it worse. Whenever people make it worse, it becomes extremely difficult to forgive them. To add to our suffering, sometimes we suffer and find it difficult to bounce back when it's not our fault. To suffer on behalf of someone else's transgressions is just as difficult, if not harder.

Remember what Jesus went through on the cross? He suffered for our sins, and each attack was worse than the previous one. They whipped Him all night long, plucked out His beard, gambled for His clothes, spat upon Him, cursed Him, gave Him vinegar to drink, placed a crown of thorns upon His head, placed nails in His hands and feet, and then pierced Him in His side! Can you imagine how hard it must have been as each physical attack became worse than the previous one, ultimately saying, "Father, forgive them"?

> Forasmuch then as Christ hath suffered for us in the flesh, arm yourselves likewise with the same mind: for he that hath suffered in the flesh hath ceased from sin.
>
> (1 Peter 4:1, KJV)

Jesus suffered for us so we would not have to ever suffer due to sin again, but it wasn't His sin that took Him to the cross. Whenever we are suffering in someone else's place or at their hands, it makes it difficult to forgive them. However, you can bounce back!

When I was in elementary school, I had a teacher who used to take a smoke break outside. She would leave for fifteen minutes or so and then return smelling like cigarettes. My teacher would leave a person to take the names of any individuals who would talk. After she would return, the student(s) who talked would be in trouble. Sometimes there were kids who were really good at getting the rest of the class to talk or laugh, so the teacher would say, "If there are any names on the list, then you all will lose time off your recess." I thought taking a kid's lunch or recess was never a good idea when I was in school! For the entire class to lose time from recess when one or two individuals performed for the class until we all started laughing made the situation even worse.

Whenever you suffer because you feel like it's someone else's fault, it seems very difficult to forgive them. We will use phrases like, "If it weren't for my mother or father," or "If my teacher would have taught me something, then I would be in a better place in life!" Suffering at the hands of others in situations that go from bad to worse are difficult to forgive and let go!

Whenever sudden trials come and the universe is not cooperating with us, we freak out. "Beloved, think it not strange concerning the fiery trial which is to try you, as though some strange thing happened unto you" (1 Peter 4:12, KJV). The fiery trial he references doesn't have to be a literal fire, but have you ever felt like you were literally on fire?

Years ago, my wife and I went through a financial mess. The bills were coming in left and right, but we had more going out than coming in on our teacher salaries. At some point, I had decided that I wasn't going to use charge cards anymore. So, with a two-year-old and a newborn at home and having all of the pride from being educated beyond my college degree, I loaded up the family lawnmower, put on my cleaning clothes, and went house to house with hopes that someone would hire me to cut their yard. Unfortunately, I had doors slammed in my face. One man even threatened to turn his dogs on me for trespassing when I knocked on his door to see if he wanted his grass cut. I remember being upset and not liking what happened to me because we were in a sudden state of need, and people around us were making it worse. However, this was the situation that God was using in our lives to teach us to bounce back! Even though we don't like the present discomfort, somehow, it's making us stronger. It's like being on a bus, and the bus driver keeps hitting all the potholes on the street. It makes you want to say, "Come on, man! You are sitting up front! Can't you go around some of this mess?" Nevertheless, no matter who you are, how old you are, how much money you have or wish you had, and whether you are from this country, another country, the old country, or down in the country, Matthew 5:45 states that God sends the rain on the just and the unjust. This means everyone will, at some time in their life, hit potholes. Furthermore, having to forgive whenever you seemingly hit potholes will make your situation even worse. Christians are not immune from suffering. Sometimes we wish the bus driver of our lives would stop hitting potholes.

1 Peter 4:12 tells us to stop thinking that it can't happen to you. In other words, "Get over the fact that this has happened to you!" Stop saying, "Why is this happening to me?" "Why is God allowing this to go on?" "Why am I going through this situation?" God is saying, "Stop being surprised and expect it!"

God is molding you into a better you.

1 Peter 5:10 (KJV) states, "But the God of all grace, who hath called us unto his eternal glory by Christ Jesus, after that ye have **suffered a while**, make you perfect, stablish, strengthen, settle you."

The troubles are really just tests. This example of pain is really an exam on problems.

Think about it:

- God is perfecting you because He is correcting you!
- God is reviving you because He is providing for you!
- God is ungluing you because He is re-newing you!

How do I bounce back?

> But rejoice, inasmuch as ye are partakers of Christ's sufferings; that, when his glo-ry shall be revealed, ye may be glad also with exceeding joy.
>
> (1 Peter 4:13, KJV)

Can you rejoice that the storm is passing over?

Can you rejoice that you are about to come out?

In 2010, my wife lost her job due to downsizing, and fourteen people were let go. In 2012, my wife and kids were in a head-on collision when they were going through a traffic light. A car turning onto the adjacent road collided with them. In 2014, my job lost a contract, and several people lost their jobs, including me. Along with these personal setbacks I experienced, there were many other traumatic events going on in society and numerous personal issues others were facing. If you aren't careful, you can become angry with God for what happened to your momma, daddy, children, health, marriage, and job. Ultimately, can you bounce back from whatever should have killed you by freely releasing people from your situation and taking a personal inventory of the fact that you are still here?

You're a survivor and an overcomer, and to this end, God wants to use your present or past situation of hurt to heal others of their pain. Don't allow this situation to define you but allow it to refine you as a person. Your ability to bounce back is based upon your spiritual understanding of your challenge and allowing God to turn your bitter situation into something bigger and better.

Think About it:

- You're still here, so your situation didn't destroy you.
- There are others going through similar or worse situations and need encouragement.
- My releasing others from what part they've played in my pain will help me to be able to help others.

5.

Moving On
Let People Go!

Daniel 6:16-19

When Barack Obama became the first African American president, it was a gigantic story. Furthermore, the appointment of the first black family in the White House was just as important. It was a pivotal time in history for all Americans, especially people of color, to achieve such greatness in American politics and live before us as our first example. People were proud to visit the Obamas' in the White House, and this family's presence shifted stigmas placed on African Americans through systems of racism and sexism that needed to come down. Even more, Mrs. Obama, a beautiful, brown woman, graced the American stage to fight for healthy living for students, amongst many other campaigns she introduced as the new first lady.

My wife and I are blessed to have two daughters. As African Americans, they needed to see the Obamas, especially Michelle, in their lifetime as people to look up to. Personally, I was never taught to worship people, even though I've highlighted people I've met throughout this book. However, I want to make it clear that I've been blessed to meet wonderful people who had low means as well as some of great affluence. At the end of the day, we're all just people.

I stayed in a hotel once in Pittsburgh while in town for a funeral. Young girls were camped out to see a glimpse of the popular boy band, *One Direction*, who was staying in the penthouse suite. At that time, *One Direction* was being compared to the same following power as the Beatles, and their popularity was mind-blowing. Similarly, I was at the AMC Empire 25 Movie Theater in Manhattan in 2013 when Hugh Jackman stood behind a velvet rope to greet movie fans on premiere night of his latest *Wolverine* movie installment. Die-hard fans wore Wolverine masks and cried as they filmed Hugh from their cell phones. On both of these occasions, I never understood the reactions of crying and screaming from the fans—I wasn't raised that way. While others honor these artists for their work, all of my worship goes to God only! However, we were several hundreds of feet away from the Obamas on two occasions, and it was surreal. To know that you were in the presence of history makers and people who were in the public eye was sort of an unbelievable thing.

The first occasion was when I brought my family to the White House Easter Egg Roll. My students and I received tickets to visit the White House lawn for this incredible event when I was an elementary school principal. The Obamas appeared from the balcony and later joined the crowd, especially during the fitness portion when the music and exercising took place.

The second occasion was in 2009, and it involved my godson playing college basketball. Calvin played on Michelle Obama's brother's basketball team, the Oregon State Beavers, and my family attended the game as Calvin's guests. We were just across the court from the Obamas, and this event went down in our family scrapbook as a magnificent moment. Whether you support the ideas and philosophies of the Obamas or not, it was evident that history was in the room. Most often, celebrities light up the rooms they are in, usually with something that is euphoric about their presence. The Obamas' presence was symbolized as a symbol of hope, including the idea of the pursuit of happiness.

If ever there was a man who let his light shine in the midst of darkness, it was Daniel. He was a man who didn't allow the corruptness of the government of his day to influence his lifestyle. Daniel was a teenager when he was taken captive during the siege and duress of Jerusalem under Babylon's wicked king, Nebuchadnezzar, and he survived under two other ungodly kings: Belshazzar and Darius. Daniel's survival reminds us that God always has a remnant for His people.

Though the world is given to drunkenness, hedonism, and people living for pleasures and doing whatever their wicked imaginations desire, God still has people who will bring hope and goodness to others. Yes, there are worldly people who are more concerned with living for the weekend and attaining number one as they selfishly trample others to make a promotion, but God still has people.

Letting People Go Is a Calling to Greatness!

Whenever you find it difficult to forgive others, remember that you have been called to greatness by helping others to see Christ in you. You are like that special family who once lived in our White House, named the Obamas, who changed the world just as much as you can.

Sometimes, the beginning point for bringing hope and light to the world is by forgiving others. You are of no benefit whenever you choose to hold on to unforgiveness. Here are three reminders from Daniel that have helped me:

1. You are favored by God.

In Daniel 6:1–3, there was great evidence of Daniel's favor by God, but at the same time, he had to forgive others. The Hebrew word for "preferred" in verse 3 means select, noticeable, distinct, and chosen. Daniel was under great persecution for being a follower of God. However, this didn't stop God's blessings for him. Therefore, people who've been blessed should become a blessing to others. How? By giving the gift of forgiveness to others. You and I have the gift of favoring others by letting them go and pardoning them for whatever they've done to us. We're to use our favor like a king or monarch who grants clemency to others, although they have done the crime. Daniel was so loved and favored by God, but it was so he could love and favor others. Do you know why you've been favored by God? It's so you can bless someone else who needs to be released from whatever they've done. On January 19, 2017, President Obama granted lesser prison sentences to 330 federal prisoners who were mainly drug offenders. These individuals were arrested and convicted for the possession of substances, which means the evidence was seized upon conviction, yet the president used his power to release them from prison. As a favored child of God, you have the power to release others from the prison sentence for whatever they've done to you.

2. You're going to need the same forgiveness that you offer to others for yourself someday.

When Daniel was unfairly arrested, he was almost pardoned because of the graciousness he was willing to give to others. However, I'm sure he went back to his room, night after night, wishing that God would vindicate him during his time of serving under restraint. Furthermore, when it was time to show love and forgive, Daniel was able to do so. Therefore, when his enemies came against him, it wasn't as bad as it could have been. Why? Because people who show mercy and forgiveness also receive it from others.

> Then the presidents and princes sought
> to find occasion against Daniel concern-
> ing the kingdom; but they could find none

occasion nor fault; forasmuch as he was faithful, neither was there any error or fault found in him. Then said these men, We shall not find any occasion against this Daniel, except we find it against him concerning the law of his God.

(Daniel 6:4–5, KJV)

The only complaint they had against Daniel was actually a compliment. Daniel was a man of God who openly prayed, and everyone knew it. For this reason, Daniel was being chastised. However, the same thing he was criticized for was a sign of Daniel's strength in God.

Can you be criticized for being a man or woman of mercy and forgiveness? Can the accusation against you be that you are loving, merciful, and forgiving? Remember, you are favored by God.

3. People will not always respect your forgiveness.

In Daniel 6:6–13, these men tried to entrap Daniel, although he never disrespected them and probably prayed for them. Not everyone is going to respect you and appreciate you, even if you treat them with love, respect, dignity, and honor. Some people will try to destroy you and even ruin your name.

When the king made the decree for anyone who was not praying to him or his false gods to be destroyed, this impacted Daniel greatly. Accusers brought Daniel to the king. By his command, Daniel was to be punished. These jealous Chaldeans got the king to create a new law that would punish people for serving the true and living God. Remember, all Daniel was doing was praying and probably for them. Daniel was doing the right thing by obeying the Lord when he was set up by men.

I want to submit to you that some of the hardest people to forgive are those who do harm to you, while you are trying to do good to them. "Yea, and all that will live godly in Christ Jesus shall suffer persecution" (2 Timothy 3:12, KJV). What this verse doesn't say is that sometimes you suffer by the hands of those whom you are trying to bless! What was Daniel doing? He was praying. Regardless of how Daniel got in trouble, he could have held onto what these men had done against him.

Be careful not to become a "people collector" when others hurt you. This type of person holds on to the people who've tried to hurt him or her. By simply living in the yesterdays of life, it can cause you to not feel like you can make it today and lose your bright hope for tomorrow. The cause of your lack of forgiveness is what someone has said or done.

Ask yourself:

- Do you forgive others who meant to do you wrong?
- Do you forgive others who meant to hurt your feelings?
- Do you forgive others who meant to embarrass you?
- Do you forgive others who meant to

destroy you?

On the other hand, are you a person who carries around what people have done to you for years? Do you want to forgive them and do not know how? Do you think you have forgiven them, but are not sure? To know if you are **healed** of an unforgiving heart, the following things can occur:

1. Your attitude changes.

Nowhere in the story of Daniel do you see that he was fazed by his accusers. Nowhere in any verse do you see Daniel bitter. Rather, he just went right along with the consequences in a humble like fashion.

You have to admit it. Some of you have let what people have done to you affect your attitude and personality. When you look in the mirror, you don't even recognize yourself at times. This is because you are so used to reacting to what people have done to you that you have developed multiple personalities (according to your reactions to what people have done). Therefore, you have a sad personality caused by years of somebody calling you ugly. You have an angry personality caused by years of somebody abusing you. You have a fearful personality of rejection caused by years of somebody hurting your feelings or calling you names.

These multiple personalities are nothing more than a collection of your reactions to people hurting you over the years. That's why sometimes you can be nice, and other times you act like you are a hostile worker in a sweatshop or on a chain gang. All it takes is the wrong word or look from another, which triggers one of your personalities to come forth due to years of dealing with people who have hurt you in your past. Moreover, depending on what day it is, we might run into the wrong personality ourselves, which can hinder us in our walk with God and how we worship him.

> Therefore if thou bring thy gift to the altar, and there rememberest that thy brother hath ought against thee; Leave there thy gift before the altar, and go thy way; first be reconciled to thy brother, and then come and offer thy gift.

> (Matthew 5:23–24, KJV)

Some of you can't even get into true worship because you are so backed up with what someone has done unto you that it's standing in the way. It's time for some of you to change your attitude. Stop hollering at total strangers who don't get your order right. Stop hollering at the cars on the road during your morning and evening commutes. Just stop hollering in general. Many times, we are hollering because we are backed up with a collection of things people have done to us. All you've got to do is stop letting what happened to you continue to change who you are now. Now is the time to refuse to let people change your mood, character, and attitude. When you release people and what they've done, then you will stop responding to your past hurts.

2. You won't let people lock you up.

In Daniel 6:16, notice the king's men brought Daniel to the lion's den and threw him in, but Daniel wasn't upset. Why? Daniel was not restricted by what these people had done to him; yet, this was still a hard thing to do for Daniel.

Forgiving others is never as easy as it may sound. We like to think that forgiveness is easy, but the reality is it's not. People can hurt you. Even though they may be dead now, if you are not careful, you can still carry them around with you. There is no hurt like a hurt from people who are now dead. At least if the person were still alive, you could ride past their house and throw eggs or place a candy bar in their gas tank, but a dead person feels nothing from you. Sometimes, all some of us have is a picture of the person who hurt us, and in the picture, they might be smiling.

Undoubtedly, it was difficult for Daniel to forgive, but he did. These men weren't just trying to get Daniel in trouble; they were trying to destroy him forever. Moreover, he was sent into the lion's den because of something somebody said. Some of you aren't in an actual lion's den but are in a liar's den because of something someone said.

I can tell you that one of the hardest things about letting go of what people have done to me is actually letting go of what people have done to me. Sometimes there is something about being the victim that is comforting to us. We like to be able to tell our story and have people come running to our aid all the time. Furthermore, we like to have people make excuses for our behavior all the time. Also, we like to be able to have people hold us up and encourage us because we are a victim. However, the problem with being a victim is that it locks you into a place where you are allowed to keep remembering what was done to you. This makes it hard to forgive others who have hurt you.

As long as you keep seeing where you were, feeling how you felt, and holding on to what they did to you, you will never have an opportunity to heal and forgive them.

Daniel lived during the time the children of Israel were in Babylonian captivity. They were supposed to be singing praises and worshiping God, but instead, they were filled with grief and sadness. However, Psalms 137:1–4 shares how the people could muster up a joyous song during their time of grief. How do you know when you are dealing with unforgiveness? Is it when you can't sing because it feels like you're in a lion's den? Today it is time to let the people go so you can sing.

> Remember ye not the former things, neither consider the things of old.
>
> (Isaiah 43:18, KJV)

You cannot spend the rest of your life driving and looking in the rearview mirror; you're going to have an accident! Furthermore, Isaiah 43:19 states that God is doing a new thing in Israel's life. This correlates to our lives now, too. All your past experiences were a set up for God to do a new thing!

What happens when some of you carry around what people have done to you? You collect people and the hurt they've given to you until it becomes unbearable. Some of you are like Lazarus in John 11:38–44, whom Jesus told to rise again, come forth out of the tomb, and stand in place to be seen by men. The interesting thing about Lazarus was that he was wrapped from head to toe in grave clothes. For this reason, he was alive but considered bound. God tells some of us to come forth and live again, but we're still bound. Jesus had to instruct the men at the tomb of Lazarus to unwrap his grave clothes so he wouldn't be bound anymore. Today, it's time to unwrap your grave clothes and leave your bondage.

In Daniel 6:17–20, Daniel slept through the night without any harm from the lions that were there to kill and eat him. Just the same, God is watching over all of us despite what people may do to us, and He keeps us through the night. All Daniel needed to do was acknowledge that he was still alive. Some of us have survived the most horrific situations and pain. Many of you have made it through abuse and mistreatment from others. Whenever you realize people can't destroy you, you can rejoice and let them go.

For those of you who made it through the night seasons of your life—years of abuse, people turning their backs on you, and people trying to destroy you—you ought to forgive those people and let them go. Even Christ said from the cross while bleeding from his wounds, "...Father, forgive them; for they know not what they do..." (Luke 23:34, KJV). If Jesus can forgive, then so can you and me.

"No weapon that is formed against thee shall prosper; and every tongue that shall rise against thee in judgment thou shalt condemn. This is the heritage of the servants of the LORD, and their righteousness is of me, saith the LORD" (Isaiah 54:17, KJV). This means every voice from your past that was sent to kill you will have to be quiet.

If It Doesn't Work for You, Then Don't Let It Work on You.

If remembering what somebody said or has done to you is not working for you, then don't let it work on you. You're actually doing better than you claim to be because no real harm has been done to you. Don't get me wrong... abuse, mistreatment, and hurt at the hands of others does physically hurt, but God has a way of protecting the human spirit and making it resilient with His support. Daniel 6:23 tells us that Daniel was not harmed in any way. Therefore, freedom is a choice. Because God has forgiven you, you ought to forgive someone else. Today, it is time to release others!

6.

Moving Out of Blame

When It's Not My Fault!

2 King 19:1-4

People are a trip! They have an interesting way of projecting their problems upon you at times and accusing you of doing what they are actually doing to you. For me, I love people with God's love. I know that we all have the ability to be obstinate, but there are some people who operate in an extra amount of foolishness.

For example, have you ever apologized to someone and they left you hanging? It's like trying to give someone a high five and they're not paying attention. You end up holding your hand out, waiting for the other person to meet your high-fived hand in the air.

Sometimes people not only fail to reciprocate your apology, but they also have a way of shifting the blame to you. Sometimes people seemingly pick you out of a lineup of good people just to mess with and make your life miserable. There is usually no apparent reason, as far as you can see, for why they chose to drive you crazy. To make matters worse, they show no remorse in doing so. It is very difficult to forgive vindictive, mean, cantankerous, and obstinate people who hurt you and then blame you for how they acted towards you.

Hezekiah was a godly king for the nation of Judah in 1 Kings, chapter 18. He tore down idols and recovered gold and silver from the temple, which was placed for materialistic means. He is known for refocusing Israel's attention upon God. He recovered gold to give it to the king of Assyria as some kind of peace offering. The people of Judah had just attacked a nation that Assyria had claimed; this was an apology, as well as an attempt to buy off this nation. The result was laughter from the armies and king of Assyria toward Hezekiah's sacrifice of gold and silver to them and threats to destroy the people of Judah. The armies and king of Assyria bragged to Hezekiah's men in verses 23 and 24 and said that they would even give the 2,000 horses to ride in battle against them, but they would still beat them!

Moreover, in chapter 19, verse 1, Hezekiah now receives the news that Assyria still threatens to take them out. 2 Kings 19:1 has Hezekiah's reaction: worry, then worship. I think it's interesting the last few words of this verse are "went into the house of the LORD" (KJV). Our response to come into the house of God during a difficult situation is critical but optional.

Some of you who are reading this book is still dealing with the pain that someone may have caused you. I mean, it's hard not to picture slapping people who have hurt you, but what you will accomplish is the feeling of separation from God due to your thought life. Like any trial in your life, it can either draw you closer to or further away from God. Therefore, a marital problem can either draw you closer to your spouse or further away. A problem at your job can either draw you closer to God and the church or further away. Today, you have to stop having mental pictures of you burning down their houses and causing people harm because it is drawing you further away from God. I will admit, there is something satisfying to our flesh about picturing our enemies being hurt for what they've done, but does your form of justice cause you to have a breach with God? Whatever we go through in life, we should allow it to become the bridge that makes us closer to God and not further away.

What draws you closer to God? Not only did Hezekiah draw closer to God, but he also wanted peace with his enemies. Why did Hezekiah really send a peace offering to the nation of Assyria and King Sennacherib? According to 2 Kings 19:13–14, King Hezekiah realized he was suddenly under attack by the King of Assyria, and he apologized, even though he had done nothing wrong to the king. He apologized to preserve peace.

Has God ever made you apologize to someone and you did nothing wrong to them? I see this kind of apology as being led by God for the purpose of promoting brother or sisterhood in Christ. This is why Hezekiah was scrambling to take gold off the palace doors and temple to give it to the King of

Assyria in verses 14–16. Some commentaries have called Hezekiah's actions a bribe. In actuality, he was trying to make matters better between the two nations, even though it backfired.

On more than one occasion in my life, God has had me sit across from someone who had done something to me. In order to preserve peace, I apologized. Unfortunately, on most of those occasions, the other person did not apologize once they received my apology. Additionally, each time I held back my emotions and kept my tears in my head. The person did absolutely nothing in their response to repair matters, although they accepted my apology. Have you ever apologized for something that you didn't do, and the other person looked at you like you were crazy? To make matters worse, you may have walked away wondering, *What did I ever do for this person to treat me so bad?* In fact, there are some people who already have it in their minds that you are the worst person in the world, and nothing you can say will change their minds or make them apologize back to you.

In 2 Kings 18:19, Hezekiah apologized, and then the King sent back a word basically saying, "Who do you think you are?" What do you do when you pour out your heart to repair a relationship problem with someone and they look at and treat you like you're crazy? Sometimes they look at you like they are thinking, *Who do you think you are?* or *Yeah, you are sorry and I want you to feel sorry,* or *You should apologize, and I was right for whatever I did to you.*

What do you do when you extend yourself to someone who does not want to forgive you, even though you messed up and apologized for it? Moreover, what do you do when you feel like you didn't do anything wrong, but they think you did, so you apologized? After you apologized, it was not received as an apology. Instead, that person would rather walk around feeling like they have the upper hand with you because they got you right where they wanted you. This may make you feel sad, sorry, depressed, or even distressed.

Some people are emboldened in their opinions about you being wrong and them being right. Sometimes they even go as far as to bring God into the situation to fit their agenda. Oftentimes, the more people side with your enemy, the more it looks like they're right to most people. In 2 Kings, chapter 18, a top soldier from the Assyrian army had a conversation with one of Hezekiah's top soldiers. Furthermore, in verse 25, the representative from the Assyrian army told the messenger to go back and tell Hezekiah God was actually on their side and not his.

Why? Because in verses 23 and 24, there were more troops with the Assyrians than for the Judeans. As a result, it looked like the Assyrians were right. Sometimes people think that because there are more people with them than with you, they must be right and you must be wrong. Just because everybody around you wants to do the wrong thing and you are standing for what's right, it doesn't mean that they must be right because you are outnumbered. If your rule of thumb for being right about something has to be everybody siding with you, you are in trouble. If you are someone who needs popular opinions to side with you so you will stand up for what you believe, you are in trouble.

God needs people who are **NOT** persuaded by popular opinions of people but instead will stand for what's right according to the word of God. Hezekiah tried to bring peace between him and another person, actually a nation, and was refused. In verses 32–35, his enemies went as far as to say that even God wouldn't deliver them. The thing I love about what happened at this point in the text is that God's name was now on the line. When someone doesn't want to forgive you and then taunts you, it's not your name on the line—it's God's.

Our reaction to being outnumbered is often fear and the idea that our strength is gone. When Hezekiah heard his offering for this nation was rejected, he responded in fear and lost strength. He actually compared that moment in 2 Kings 19:3 to a woman who is in full labor but doesn't have enough strength to push the baby out during delivery.

I believe that many of us are tired of people's shenanigans to the point where there is no strength in us and fear overtakes us. When people don't forgive us and treat us like we did something wrong, it makes our rest interrupted. You don't have to be unable to sleep at night in order to be considered restless. Whenever your mind is constantly focused upon what someone has done to you and how vindictive they have become, it makes your rest interrupted. Nothing removes your strength like attacks from your enemies, and nothing restores your strength like worship to the Lord. When we serve a God, who inhabits the praises of His people and you stop worshipping Him, you remove yourself from being intimate with God. Any person, trial, circumstance, and/or situation that is intending to stop your worship of God is not of God. Therefore, what we have to do is get to the place where we are involved in real worship to God on a continuous basis.

Real Worship Has Nothing to Do with You and What's Going on with You.

Real worship is when you can't find any reason other than who God is to worship. On the other hand, when you say, "Lord, I'll worship you while I'm catching the bus to work, and I'll worship you with a new car," this makes you become a conditional worshipper.

David said, "I will bless the LORD at all times: his praise shall continually be in my mouth. My soul shall make her boast in the LORD: the humble shall hear thereof, and be glad. Oh, magnify the LORD with me, and let us exalt his name together. I sought the LORD, and he heard me, and delivered me from all my fears" (Psalms 34:1–4, KJV). David removed the conditions from his worship to God, although he was on the run from his enemies.

I remember when one of my daughters was born after my wife's water broke in the hospital. The doctors were scurrying around, trying to get it together and help her deliver the baby. Once the water broke, there was only so much time before the child would be delivered or suffer life-threatening damages inside the womb. What helped my wife deliver the baby was her restored excitement that we could almost see our daughter during the process. When you begin to worship God, your strength becomes renewed, and you stop focusing upon the pain. It's time to stop being distracted by people and focus upon God instead.

Don't worry about:

- People who don't like you!
- People who won't forgive you!
- People who make you feel like dirt!

God was strengthening and toughening Hezekiah, and He's doing the same for you. God is getting ready to change your situation, but He needs you to toughen up. Don't worry about the person who doesn't see their wrongs and won't apologize to you. Instead, focus on your change. Hezekiah was so far out there by standing up to the challenges of the Assyrians. He believed that God was going to fight for the people of Judah, or they were about to lose the battle.

One of the reasons you don't apologize to people and shift the guilt and pain to us is that we are afraid of how we're going to feel. We need to become like Hezekiah and cancel our contingency plans in order to get this off of us. Hezekiah needed a breakthrough, and it was not going to happen because of a peace treaty between Judah and the Assyrians. Stop rehearsing in your mind that the other person is going to admit to what they've done or apologize because you don't need it in order to become whole again.

In 2 Kings 19:4, Hezekiah referred to the people of God as his remnant or covered and protected ones. All you have to do is realize that whatever tried to kill you didn't work, and you're actually better because of this. All Hezekiah had to do was recognize that whatever was done to him didn't work because he was still standing.

How Did It End for the People of Judah?

> And it came to pass that night, that the angel of the LORD went out, and smote in the camp of the Assyrians an hundred fourscore and five thousand: and when they arose early in the morning, behold, they were all dead corpses.

> (2 Kings 19:35, KJV)

Get your focus off of the fight and how bad it looks today because God will fight your battles for you! It's time to develop the gift of "leave it alone". You never read where Hezekiah tried to go back to the Assyrians to plead with them. Instead, he left it alone, and God took care of it.

God Has Had Me Forgive People Who Didn't Forgive Me.

One time I was trying to find the end of the line in a store. I saw an endless sea of people. As I was walking near the line, there was a frustrated man with his two children. As I walked past him, he backed up and we bumped each other. I quickly apologized for bumping into him. To my surprise, as he looked up at me, it was like he was going to hit me. All I saw was red in his eyes. However, I pleaded with him to forgive me, although I felt it was his fault. What I was asking him to do was to forgive me for whatever he felt I had done that made him so angry. Here's how God helped me with that moment. I could hear God saying to me, "What did you come into this store for?" Well, the answer was simply to get some things and then get out. In other words, God wanted me to refocus my attention on Him.

Today, some of you need to get your focus back and take your eyes off this or that person. Just do what God sent you to do, and don't worry about the people in it. Regain your focus back on God. You don't need the other person to apologize in order to move on. When it is not your fault, don't worry about whose fault it is and let the other person go. Letting people go is one of the most liberating things you can ever do with your life. Make a list of all the people who harmed you and decide that today, you are letting them all go!

7.

Moving on with Yourself
Talk to the Good Part of You!

Romans 8:11-15

As you are reading this book, there is a part of you that wants to read and hear advice like this, and there's another part of you who doesn't. Seriously, there is still a part of all of us that wants to destroy our enemies and people who tried to destroy us. However, you have to tell the part of you that wants to move on that unforgiveness is harming you. As long as you harbor hurt, you will continue to feed the part of you that doesn't want to forgive. If you can still vividly see yourself slapping someone, then you might be somehow feeding the part of you that is still hurting.

There is a part of you that wants to hurt the people who hurt you, and there's another part of you that wants to forgive them. If we're honest with ourselves, there are two different parts of us that are at war; the part of us that we feed the most will always win the fight. I would be lying if I said that forgiving people is both easy and something that you will willingly do. The truth is that most of the time, we don't want to forgive someone. We feel justified in what we are thinking and feeling about the individual. It takes a level of maturity to do the things you don't want to do. When you grow up in your mind, things will become easier. For example, usually kids run and play all day long, but at the end of the day, they don't want to bathe. It's only through discipline and teaching them to enjoy bath time that bathing becomes routine and not even a thought anymore.

Are You at War with Yourself?

Until you conquer the bad part (flesh) of you, you will always give in to it. This will cause you to miss an opportunity to grow. When I talk with Christians, I am always surprised by how many have very little time for God, but somehow, they are always promoting their maturity in the faith. Most times, they are promoting how they feel. Sometimes, we over spiritualize our situation by assigning God to our feelings. If we don't feel like doing something (even if it's good), we assume that it must be God telling us not to do it. The entitled part of you that wants to lie around and nurse your fleshly desires will win. You will not forgive people if you are a person who lives according to how you feel or what you believe you're entitled to.

You will also limit your exposure by giving in to what you feel rather than what God's word tells us we should do. Forgiveness is one of those things that requires you to remove your feelings, entitlements, and sense of judgments and check your emotions at the door. This will not always feel like the right thing to do, though. You have to be committed to your destiny enough to leave people in the past who have tried to kill your dreams, poison your outlook, and ruin your life. These people do not deserve the time and energy you will spend mulling over whether you should even address them.

Do what the Bible says and forgive them quickly. Then, keep it moving! Don't spend another second, minute, hour, day, week, month, or a year thinking about what someone did to you. Learn the gift of quick forgiveness and keeping it moving. This person doesn't deserve to make your life miserable for an evening or the next twenty years of your life. Let them go and put them in the proper place where they belong. You have to renew your mind quickly to let things go. I can't tell you how many countless hours it takes for me to renew my mind. Mind renewal has to be an uninterrupted and ongoing process. You have to make an investment in yourself in order to have the sacrificial and self-effacing commitment it takes for one to renew his or her mind. If you are going to put to death anything from your past and walk in the new you, you must renew your mind!

> For I know that in me (that is, in my
> flesh) dwelleth no good thing...
>
> (Romans 7:18, KJV)

The early church kept the teachings of Jesus alive in their hearts and minds in order to embrace a new covenant. If you are going to experience something fresh and new, like being able to forgive someone, then you need to embrace a renewed mind and obey the Spirit of God. Below are examples of the old covenant compared to the new one:

In Leviticus, chapters 4–7, in the Old Testament, the priest was to take the sins of Israel and atone them in the temple or tabernacle by making a blood sacrifice of a dove, pigeon, goat, bull, or heifer. The priest would have to sprinkle the sacrifice's blood seven times on the mercy seat. This annual act forgave the Jews of their sins for a year. However, in the New Testament, Jesus' sacrifice was meant to be a permanent atonement. Jesus' act of mercy on our behalf showed His unlimited extension of God the Father's love and grace towards us. Therefore, even before Jesus went to the cross for our sins, He explained to His disciples how infinite forgiveness should be based upon the future sacrifice He would make and no longer a focus on the Old Testament law.

Jesus was asked, "...Lord, how oft shall my brother sin against me, and I forgive him? Till seven times?" (Matthew 18:21, KJV). Notice the question contains the number seven and is a direct reference to the Jewish Law of Moses. Jesus replied, "...Unto him, I say not unto thee, Until seven times: but, Until seventy times seven" (Verse 22). Jesus was implying that forgiveness should occur an infinite number of times. Again, Jesus understood the difficulty in forgiving others when He shared His response to the question prior to going to the cross to atone our infinite sin with His infinite love, grace, and mercy.

In the Old Testament, the high priest was commanded to bring two goats together. "Aaron shall cast lots upon the two goats..." (Leviticus 16:8, KJV). One of the goats was going to be brought into the temple to be a sacrifice for their sins, and the other goat was going to be released in the wilderness to be eaten by wild animals as a means of being judged by the Lord. However, in the New Testament, John the Baptist was in Bethabara beyond the river Jordan while he was baptizing new converts, he looked up and saw Jesus coming. Notice Jesus' response, "... Behold the Lamb of God, which taketh away the sin of the world" (John 1:29, KJV).

In the Old Testament in Exodus, chapters 25 and 26, God told the first church how to build the tabernacle. This was to be done with the mercy seat on the ark of the covenant by sprinkling the blood of animals on it to atone the sins of Israel in the Old Testament. However, Jesus came along later in the New Testament and stated,

> Neither by the blood of goats and calves, but by his own blood he entered in once into the holy place, having obtained eternal redemption for us. For if the blood of bulls and of goats, and the ashes of an heifer sprinkling the unclean, sanctifieth to the purifying of the flesh: How much more shall the blood of Christ, who through the eternal Spirit offered himself without spot to God, purge your conscience from dead works to serve the living God?

MICHAEL A. WILSON

(Hebrews 9:12–14, KJV)

In the Old Testament, God told the Jews, concerning their enemies,

"To me belongeth vengeance, and recompence; their foot shall slide in due time: for the day of their calamity is at hand, and the things that shall come upon them make haste" (Deuteronomy 32:35, KJV). On the other hand, in the New Testament, Jesus came along. While hanging on the cross for our sins, "...Father, forgive them; for they know not what they do..." (Luke 23:34, KJV).

Do you get the point? Jesus ushered in a new covenant with new hopes and opportunities for us. The Jews were keeping the law, and its tenants when Jesus came and offered something more than righteousness by their works. As a replacement, Jesus offered the way to overcome and defeat our flesh. This is done by the entrance of the Holy Spirit into our lives, activating God's Word. The point is to reveal to us that God's way is always better than ours.

Moreover, the example of the old covenant in the Old Testament versus the new covenant found in the New Testament is to point us to the fact that God wants to improve our lives, just like His offering and plan to us improved:

- In the Old Testament God's plan was revealed, but in the New Testament God's plan was fulfilled.
- In the Old Testament God's plan was described, but in the New Testament God's plan was prescribed.

- In the Old Testament God's plan was proclaimed, but in the New Testament God's plan was arranged.

Therefore, if crying and being upset for another year is working for you, then hold on to unforgiveness. If being frantic at the sound of someone's name or hoping and praying that you will not run into that person is working, then keep doing what you're doing! However, if you're ready to release that person and do something better, then it's time to renew your mind, begin to forgive, and embrace the newness of life you now have in Christ!

Before you can acknowledge that God's plan for forgiveness is better than how you're living, you must first acknowledge that you need the forgiveness of God. No matter who you are, what you've done, where you've been, and how long it's been, you need to accept the forgiveness of God. You may not be convinced right now, but at some point, you broke the laws of God and hurt His heart.

Romans, chapters 1–3, is about everyone's need for the forgiveness of God. Within these three chapters, there are three types of people who need God's forgiveness:

1. The first type of person to forgive is the heathen man. Romans 1:18–32 refers to this type of person is someone who has said there is no God and lives according to his pleasures, showing they believe there is no God by how they live. If you're a heathen man or woman, then you need God's

love and forgiveness.

2. The second type of person to forgive is the moral man. Romans 2:1–16 refers to this type of man as one who said he is only subject to his conscience, and if it feels good, then he will do it. A moral person relies upon situational ethics and their own sense of judgment. Because they don't commit obvious sins, they think they are better the heathen man. If you're a moral man or woman, you need God's love and forgiveness.

3. The third type of person to forgive is the religious man. Romans 2:17–3:8 refers to this man as someone who thinks he is okay because he goes to church and puts money in the offering plate. This man also thinks he is going to heaven because he sings in the choir. By focusing on religious efforts to cover his sins, the religious man can never do enough to rid himself of sin. If you're a religious man or woman, you need God's love and forgiveness.

Of course, we could add a fourth man: the Christian who has already given his or her life to Christ, but sins daily and makes mistakes. We are all in need of God's love and forgiveness, and Romans 8 reminds us of this need. Check out this quick outline of the chapters leading up to chapter 8 and how they relate to forgiveness:

• Romans, chapters 4–5, is about God's

awesome plan and the creation of it.

- Romans, chapters 6–7, is about Jesus' auspicious participation in God's plan for God's forgiveness.
- Romans, chapter 8, is about the Holy Spirit's amazing provision for our walking in God's forgiveness.

The only way you're going to be able to forgive others is with a renewed mind and through the power of the Holy Spirit. When you accept God's forgiveness for yourself, you are then able to forgive others. The part of you who sees your past suffering and what was done to you will help grow your maturity and faith in God, who is ready to forgive now!

Help Yourself by Becoming Your Best!

For I reckon that the sufferings of this present time are not worthy to be compared with the glory which shall be revealed in us.

(Romans 8:18, KJV)

Every single drop of your suffering has had God's purpose in it—the purpose to push you further into your purpose and reveal God's glory. The apostle talked about the suffering we go through and how it cannot be compared to the end goal or outcome of God's glory in your life. What is God allowing you to go through that might reveal His glory further along in your life?

Do you know that there are people who

thought they hurt you and left you for dead, but actually did you a favor? They were able to push you into the presence of God by their hurts towards you. What do you do while you are still suffering and going through difficulties with this person? I feel as though I've forgiven them. But, while I am waiting for the situation to change, they are still hurting me every time I see or interact with them.

Paul says, "For the earnest expectation of the creature waiteth for the manifestation of the sons of God" (Romans 8:19, KJV). Paul says you are waiting for the manifestation of what God has already spoken into being to come to past. However, some of you are still waiting for God to vindicate you in a situation. You may be reading this book and thinking, *As soon as I go to court, get a judgment in my favor, or can see the downfall of my enemies, I can forgive this person and move on.* However, the reality is that Paul was saying to get excited about what God is doing internally in us and not just externally for our situation. Paul was saying to get excited about God giving you a new you.

Literally, this passage is about the new body we will receive in heaven someday. Until then, we will grow and have pains that are indescribable. Therefore, Paul writes to encourage and tell them that the end manifestation will be worth the hassle they endured. Just the same, whatever you get on the other side of your situation as an outcome of waiting on the Lord, it is always better than what you thought you lost from people in your situation.

Moreover, in the interim, there is an old you

that doesn't want to forgive others. You can place all your excitement upon the future and there will be a new you someday. The problem with you still being in this earthly body is that every now and then, you have to ask God to deliver you from yourself. The fleshly, unredeemed part of you is your mind that needs to be renewed; otherwise, it will curse out people and hold them down for hurting you. Every time some of you begin to walk in God's forgiveness and healing, someone tries to get you back into the pain. Sometimes, this act works for us because there is a part of us that does not want to forgive. But that part of us has also managed to hijack the reward system in our brain. Every behavior we have generates some kind of payoff or reward, and the justification of our negative feelings, thoughts, and actions is an unforgiving heart.

What is it about holding on to unforgiveness that still works for you? What is it about harboring hurt from years of what people have done to you works for you? What is it about holding onto the mess of yesterday or the day before working for you? You wouldn't do this if it didn't work for you somehow, right? While we may be quick to say, "I've forgiven someone," the evidence that you are still battling unforgiveness, "For we know that the whole creation groaneth and travaileth in pain together until now" (Romans 8:22, KJV). Because some of you are groaning, travailing, moaning, and living in agony, it is a sign that your flesh is in a battle with your spirit. Even deeper, your heart is in a fight with your mind, and it still needs to be renewed.

Therefore, the problem is not the people who did this to you. Surprisingly, you are the problem. Because there is a part of you that loves God with all of your heart, there is also a part of you that has become crucified daily.

I Want to Do This, but...

Years ago, I was a speaker at a youth retreat. There were one hundred kids at the altar at the end of the message. They were crying, praying, and calling out to God. Some accepted Christ, while others rededicated their lives. After the three-hour service, the youth returned to their cabins for lights out, but several handfuls of young people decided to go outside and play at 1:00 in the morning. Even though no one was engaged in any sexual behaviors or anything inappropriate, they were still outside and had been warned to return to their cabins a number of times. Every youth signed the youth retreat handbook, which states that campers are not to go outside and hang out after lights out. Unfortunately, some did not follow the rules and did it anyway. Because there was a real part of them that wanted to serve God that weekend, there was another part of them that said, "Whatever, I'll do what I want to do!"

There is a real part of you that wants to serve the Lord and forgive others who've hurt you. On the other hand, there is another part of you who says, "I don't care if that person dies for what they did to me." The way you overcome your flesh is that you have to dislike that part of you and stop feeding it.

Have you ever been hated by your flesh? Until you hate that part of you, you will continue to make strange bedfellows with the unforgiving part of you.

"For they that are after the flesh do mind the things of the flesh; but they that are after the Spirit the things of the Spirit" (Romans 8:5, KJV). You have to hate that part of you and stop giving attention, time, activities, words, and life to your flesh. You have to renew your mind and even possibly move away from people who promote your flesh. Are you ready to admit that there is a struggle or tug of war between your flesh and your spirit?

> But every man is tempted, when he is drawn away of his own lust, and enticed. Then when lust hath conceived, it bringeth forth sin: and sin, when it is finished, bringeth forth death.
>
> (James 1:14–15, KJV)

Every now and then, some of you struggle with something that you know you shouldn't be wrestling with, like unforgiveness. Unforgiveness can be something very subtle at first, but eventually, it begins to eat at you and can even spread to other people. Do you realize that there are nations at war that are trying to wipe each other out due to unforgiveness? There are whole armies of people that are dying all because two individuals decided they would overthrow each other instead of one forgiving the other. Consequently, whole nations of people are suffering all because the two leaders of the nations could not get past what they did to each other.

99

Who Are You at War With?

Is it your spouse, family, coworkers, or your employer? Unforgiveness has a way of growing into division and choosing sides, as well as creating lines, which are drawn for battles and wars. Now, all of a sudden, there is a division between all your people and all their people; this is all because someone didn't forgive someone. Are you getting how ridiculous this is, even though it happens all the time?

Are you a person who holds onto things too long? "For I acknowledge my transgressions: and my sin is ever before me" (Psalm 51:3, KJV). In other words, David states in this passage that he could not shake whatever he had done.

When you acknowledge that you hold onto things too long, it makes you sick of YOU. Have you ever been frustrated with your own words, attitude, and thoughts? Do you believe it is too late to change? God has been getting you ready for the biggest miracle you've ever seen in your life. What you think may take years of counseling and even someone apologizing to you, God is going to do it quickly for you.

Are you ready to forgive? Here is the secret: God is helping you to forgive people who need your forgiveness so that they may understand God's forgiveness towards them. When you forgive others, they'll know that if you can forgive them for the little thing they've done to you, then certainly God can forgive them for the gigantic thing they've done to Him.

...For unto whomsoever much is given, of

him shall be much required: and to whom
men have committed much, of him they
will ask the more.

(Luke 12:48, KJV)

I remember being hurt by a past church member. After six years of being hurt by this person, God told me to go find him. Therefore, I found this person, and he was acting as if nothing ever happened. After five minutes of talking about our families, I decided to break down the problem for him. My words were, "If there is anything I've done that led you to mistreat me, then I apologize." Ultimately, this person accepted my apology but never said the same thing to me. I don't know what I could have ever done to be treated so badly by this person in the past, but after I apologized to him, I drove home feeling free. There are some people who need to experience God's forgiveness through you because what they've done to you, they actually did to God.

What Do You Do If You've Never Seen Anyone Forgive in Your Family?

For we are saved by hope: but hope that is seen is not hope: for what a man seeth, why doth he yet hope for? But if we hope for that we see not, then do we with patience wait for it.

(Romans 8:24–25, KJV)

Some of you are finding it hard to forgive

someone because you have never seen it with your own eyes. You may have only seen examples of people in your family getting even with someone who has crossed them. Therefore, because you have not seen it with your own eyes, it makes it hard to believe you can actually forgive someone.

Some of you have a long list of relatives or people you know who do not believe in forgiving other people. However, just because you haven't seen it doesn't mean that God can't do it. "But as it is written, Eye hath not seen, nor ear heard, neither have entered into the heart of man, the things which God hath prepared for them that love him" (1 Corinthians 2:9, KJV). You are going to have to use faith and actually picture yourself sitting across from the person that mistreated you. See yourself looking them in the eye without having any bitterness in your heart or feeling funny because they are in your presence. Can you see yourself feeling comfortable being around someone that tried to destroy you? If so, you need to get a mental portrait of yourself forgiving them by renewing your mind.

Do you remember Jesus at the last supper? He was sitting across from Judas, the man who was going to sell Him out for thirty pieces of silver. In John, chapter 13, Jesus didn't blink His eyes, lower His head, or fiddle with His sandals to let them know that he wanted Judas to be dealt with. I believe that Jesus looked Judas in the eyes, sat up straight without any animosity in His heart, and said, *One of you will betray me. The one who dips his bread tonight while I dip my bread (John 13:26).* Judas knew that

Jesus knew it was him, so Jesus leaned forward and said to Judas, "What you are about to do, do quickly" (John 13:27, NIV).

Why would Jesus say this to him? Jesus already knew the end of the story. However, he still had faith to allow this man to turn him over, even though he hadn't committed any wrongdoings. It takes faith to see all that. Some of you are having a rough time because you are walking by what you see, instead of what you know. Today, put your faith into action and don't cry another day. Don't sit in your living room with the lights out at 3:00 in the morning crying and looking at old pictures. What's done is done. Now, get up in the morning and declare yourself healed so you can be set free from unforgiveness by faith in the name of Jesus.

What Do You Need to Do?

1. Change your mouth.

> Likewise the Spirit also helpeth our infirmities: for we know not what we should pray for as we ought: but the Spirit itself maketh intercession for us with groanings which cannot be uttered. And he that searcheth the hearts knoweth what is the mind of the Spirit, because he maketh intercession for the saints according to the will of God.
>
> (Romans 8:26–27, KJV)

Some of you are not yet healed from having an unforgiving spirit because you keep trying to talk to the people who hurt you. You are thinking that if you groan and utter your words of disappointment and how they wronged you, then you will feel better. You may think that if you get them to see what they've done, then they'll admit how they hurt you, and you'll be healed instantly of unforgiveness. However, God doesn't need you to talk to them. He wants you to talk Him. God doesn't need you to talk to your friends, family, or foes who hurt you. God wants you to talk to your Father, which art in Heaven.

Unfortunately, the people who hurt you may never see and admit what they've done to you. They may never say, "I'm sorry, forgive me," or, "I messed up your life for a moment!" Therefore, when you talk to God, tell Him everything that you want Him to know about how you feel. This is not the time to hold back. Provide every detail to God, so He can help you get over it. When you get through crying and talking to God, understand, on that day, God understands you. He understands your prayers, moans, laments, and wailings.

2. Change your movement.

And we know that all things work together for good to them that love God, to them who are the called according to his purpose.

(Romans 8:28, KJV)

Because you believe that God is actually working things out for you and healing you, you can behave differently. "But love ye your enemies, and do good, and lend, hoping for nothing again; and your reward shall be great, and ye shall be the children of the Highest: for he is kind unto the unthankful and to the evil" (Luke 6:35, KJV). God wants you be a blessing to someone that's hurt you.

Do you want to know when you are healed? When you can call your ex and tell him or her that you are praying for them! Do you want to know when you are healed? When you talked to the people who've wronged you and give them what they really need, which is Jesus! Do you want to know when you are healed? When you can take your focus off the people who hurt you and place your focus upon God! This is a way to bless them as if you are blessing God.

> Give, and it shall be given unto you; good measure, pressed down, and shaken together, and running over, shall men give into your bosom. For with the same measure that ye mete withal it shall be measured to you again.
>
> (Luke 6:38, KJV)

It's just a matter of time for what you've sown to come back to you. You are sowing supernatural seeds to combat seeds that were planted against you, and your ability to forgive means that you are about to step into a blessing. Can you bless your ex? There's a real struggle within to obey the part of you that wants to serve God; this other part of you must win by you feeding your spirit with positive things. Talk to the good part of you and tell him or her that "Today, we embrace the new person we are in Christ!" It's time to forgive and live.

> For I am persuaded, that neither death, nor life, nor angels, nor principalities, nor powers, nor things present, nor things to come, Nor height, nor depth, nor any other creature, shall be able to separate us from the love of God, which is in Christ Jesus our Lord.

(Romans 8:38–39, KJV)

This means you can't be separated from the final resolution of your situation because God has already given you the victory. Whatever someone has done to you, it can't stop you from receiving the love of God. Now, go and walk in forgiveness!

Conclusion

Moving into the Movement
Join the Movement!

Matthew 21

When I was about ten years old, my mother allowed me to bring my bicycle with me in the back of our station wagon to her girlfriend's house. After all, it was a Saturday morning. She was running errands, so my trusty bike went with us to her friend's house.

My mom's friend had a son who was a little younger than me. The plan was for us to ride our bikes in his neighborhood. I was from a Maryland town a couple of cities away from the Washington, D.C. line. I was certainly familiar with the area where we rode our bicycles, having grown up not too far away. As we made our way to the crab truck on our bicycles, we were called out to by a group of guys who insisted that we give them our money. I couldn't believe we were going to be robbed. I took off quickly on my bike and told my mom's friend's son, "Hit it! Let's roll!" When I got to the end of the block and turned around, they had him captive and took his things. I couldn't leave him behind to get robbed. Moreover, what was I going to tell his momma? Therefore, I went back to where the robbery was happening and ended up getting robbed with him. Then, the final feeling of violation kicked in as we peddled away on our bikes, which the robbers allowed us to keep. I couldn't believe that I had been robbed, but I was more upset with my riding partner than the robbers. Surely, I should have a pass for not forgiving them. But God isn't into unforgiveness like we are.

If you are reading this book and somehow think you are off the hook for forgiving others, you are mistaken. Jesus looks for forgiveness and was the greatest example of forgiving and moving on. In Mark, chapter 11, Jesus made it clear to the disciples when He was teaching them about prayer that God would only hear and answer the prayers of those with a forgiving heart.

Unforgiveness always does more to the person who refuses to forgive than the person who should be forgiven. When Jesus was describing the act of forgiveness to the disciples, it almost seemed like an easy thing to do. Undoubtedly, Jesus told the disciples in Mark, chapter 11, to do something that was incredibly difficult. He said to come to God in faith through prayer, but get all the unforgiveness out of your heart first. Jesus says, *Don't let anyone or anything cause your prayers to become hindered by having a heart that is full of unforgiveness!* (Mark 11:25–26). Furthermore, He stated that God would allow your prayers to become prayers that rise no higher than this ceiling, yet somehow miss going all the way to heaven because you choose to have a heart of unforgiveness.

I know what you're thinking as you hold this book and curl your toes under a throw blanket or sit on your porch and listen to the birds' chirp. You thought you were going to get to the end of it and feel better about forgiving someone, but the reality is you might not feel better. In fact, you may not even want to do what I have written about, but the benefits of forgiveness are always bigger than the challenge of the act of forgiving.

When we hold on to what people have done to us, it hinders our ability to walk in faith. Sin may not close your mouth, but it deafens God's ear. A good father knows the request of his children. However, a great father knows not to give you things when you are wrong. Therefore, whenever we expect God to bless us while we are in a mess, we think we own God. Actually, we owe God because God does not bless mess. There are a lot of people who have allowed the foolishness of their hearts to make them somehow think that God is going along with them and will still bless them. You are somehow fooling yourself into thinking that God owes you something and that you don't have to change the position or condition of your heart.

When I was growing up, my parents used to give my siblings and me chores. Every week we were responsible for cleaning something around the house. My brother James cleaned the steps and the bathrooms, and my sister Michele vacuumed the floors and cleaned all the mirrors. We all took out the trash, but we all had to take turns doing the dishes. This was our leverage for asking for things from our parents. We did not come to our parents without first doing our chores.

All Jesus told the disciples to do was keep a heart that was free from unforgiveness when they would ask something of their heavenly Father. Because of this, there are three stages of our lives that Jesus saw when He made these statements to His disciples:

First, He saw the future. Jesus had not gone to the cross yet, so for what was He possibly forgiving folks? Jesus knew He was going to the cross in the future and was telling the disciples to prepare their minds for whatever may come in your future. He was later falsely accused, imprisoned, punished, and beaten before He was crucified on a cross. Jesus, in His human experience, didn't know exactly who was going to sell Him out unless the Father told Him that His own people would run to the Roman officials about Him. However, Jesus forgave them. Who do you need to forgive because they have the potential of selling you out? Your own people may possibly turn on you, but build a spirit of forgiveness for them into your heart right now.

Second, forgive people for what they are currently doing to you. As Jesus rode into Jerusalem in Matthew, chapter 21, He knew that the people who praised Him were also going to curse Him. Jesus felt this so badly later as He saw their sin and wept for them in Matthew 23:37–39. Have you ever cried for someone who hurt you? "Ye are of God, little children, and have overcome them: because greater is he that is in you, than he that is in the world" (1 John 4:4, KJV). This means what people think they're doing to us is also something they're doing to themselves. You have to make a decision not to let the people destroy you or stop you from enjoying your life. Don't let them force you to act out of character and snap. Stop picturing removing their weave or hitting them so hard that you fade their hair on the sides. No, forgive them for what they are doing.

The challenge we have with forgiving people in real-time is not allowing them to keep doing whatever they are currently doing to us. Forgiveness doesn't mean that I keep letting you do to me whatever you're doing. It's one thing to forgive a person for what they are doing, but it's another thing to stand there and let that person keep doing it to you. If I keep letting someone do something to me over and over again, it is no longer his or her fault. It is now my fault. Somewhere along the line, some of you have to forgive yourselves for what you keep letting people do to you over and over again. You don't have to stay in the presence of someone who keeps abusing you in order to prove that you've forgiven them.

When I was in elementary school, I had a buddy who had all the latest toys. If you were lucky enough to play with him, you had to use his bad or broken toys. Sometimes, we played good guys and bad guys or cops and robbers, and he always made me the bad guy or robber. Eventually, I said, "Enough is enough!" I took a break and stopped playing with him. It wasn't what he was doing to me; it was what I was letting him do to me. Again, there are some things that are hard to forgive because we need to forgive ourselves for what we keep letting someone do to us. You can let other people off the hook for what they are presently doing when you realize that some of it is your fault for letting them hurt you again and again. "Keep thy heart with all diligence; for out of it are the issues of life" (Proverbs 4:23, KJV). Therefore, I forgive others for what they've done, but I also protect my heart from letting them do this over and over again!

Third, Jesus says to forgive people for what they have done to us in the past. Can you forgive people for how they have troubled you? In Matthew 14:1–12, the same Roman soldiers who hung Jesus had already killed His cousin, John the Baptist. In Matthew 2:13–16, even King Herod, at the time Jesus was born, tried to kill Him before He was even born.

Can you imagine what Jesus was telling the disciples to let go of? When Jesus was born, He was already on the run. He was already in trouble before He spoke His first words or walked His first steps. His coming to earth was a struggle all alone. Maybe you know what it is like to be born into a struggle. You know what it is like to come to earth already in trouble because of poverty, your family, or generational curses. Maybe papa was a rolling stone or momma was single and unhappy. Whatever the reasons, you may have been birthed into situations beyond your control. There may have been some fights that started before you were born, and now you have to address them as a survivor.

As a survivor, put the past behind you to save yourself a world of headaches. You can ask God to help you as He promised, "Thou wilt keep him in perfect peace, whose mind is stayed on thee: because he trusteth in thee" (Isaiah 26:3, KJV). You should refuse to hold on to all the mess from your past because the Bible says, "Hope deferred maketh the heart sick..." (Proverbs 13:12, KJV). You can make yourself sick holding on to disappointments. You may end up missing your dreams and opportunities because you are holding on to letdowns from your past. You cannot move forward if you keep looking backward! Moreover, before you move on with your life, forgive everyone from your past. If holding on to what people have done is causing you to miss what God said He would do, then let every last person go who may have hurt you so you can be free.

Brethren, I count not myself to have apprehended: but this one thing I do, forgetting those things which are behind, and reaching forth unto those things which are before, I press toward the mark for the prize of the high calling of God in Christ Jesus.

(Philippians 3:13–14, KJV)

Let it go and always remember:

I know it's easier said than done, but let it go!

I know you feel justified, but let it go!

I know it makes sense to hold on to it, but let it go!

I know you feel like you're right, but let it go!

God's release for you comes whenever you release what people have done to you. How do you know when you have really forgiven people? When you let go of whatever they've done to you in the past!

Once, I was so angry with this student who was supposed to be my friend. Here I was in a sixth-grade classroom, and I was furious enough to fight him. My friend from our neighborhood was egging me on to fight in the classroom. My teacher had previously announced to tell her the next time someone wanted to fight, and she would bring in boxing gloves. Therefore, I told the teacher that I needed her to bring in those boxing gloves because I was ready to throw down! To my surprise, my teacher kept me from fighting my classmate. I forgave him and moved on.

That summer, the same student murdered one of my fellow bandmates in the street around the corner from our house. What I was previously angry about could have resulted in an altercation that actually could have taken my life instead of my bandmate's. I never knew that this event was going to continue to impact me when people would do things to me later in my life. I realized that holding on to lies, rumors, and mistreatment could result in my death somehow. People attempt to kill your joy, peace, love, patience, and outlook for life whenever we hold on to what they do.

Jesus was doing more than encouraging His disciples to quit being twelve angry men. He was empowering them to forgive others quickly, so they would still be able to embrace their futures. Do you know that the thing you won't let go of and the person you choose not to forgive is actually killing you on the inside? Some people are dying slowly with anger, while others die with frustration. Jesus said, *I guarantee you that your prayers will be heard, but also hindered as long as you are holding on to something in your heart!* Therefore, join the movement of forgiveness and let people go! Your glorious future doesn't need to be hindered by your past. Forgiveness doesn't minimize your past; it enlarges your future. It's time to forgive and move on!

Join the movement today and also take the "forgiveness test" at: www.forgivenessmovement. com

References

"Harlem by Langston Hughes." 2019. Poetry Foundation. 2019. https://www.poetryfoundation.org/poems/46548/harlem.

"Strong's Greek: Issue." 2019. Biblhub. 2019. https://biblehub.com/greek/4511.htm.

The Holy Bible: King James Version [KJV]. 1999. New York: American Bible Society. Public Domain. https://www.biblegateway.com/versions/King-James-Version-KJV-Bible/#booklist

The Holy Bible: New International Version [NIV]. 1984. Grand Rapids: Zondervan Publishing House. https://www.biblegateway.com/versions/New-International-Version-NIV-Bible/#booklist

About the Author

Michael A. Wilson is the son of Rev. James Wilson, Sr. and Mrs. Diane Wilson (founder of Sister's Keepers International and Uniting Sisters). He is the proud husband of Mrs. Rachel Wilson and the father of two lovely daughters, Jordan and Jayda. He has been married to his college sweetheart and wife for over twenty years.

Consecutively, he's been involved in ministry and public education for over twenty years as a pastor, counselor, school principal, college professor, and nonprofit director. He has completed coursework at George Washington University, Harvard University, Howard University, Bowie State University, Columbia University, and Trinity College (DC). He also holds a BS in Youth Studies from Liberty University, a Masters in Education from Regent University, a Doctorate of Ministry from Calvary Christian College, and a Doctorate in Pastoral Counseling from ATS Seminary.

Michael holds degrees in youth studies, education, ministry, and pastoral counseling. He is also a veteran of the U.S. Army reserves and has volunteered with numerous nonprofit boards, jails, hospitals, nursing homes, schools, and a hospice house.

He credits his ministry success to sitting under the great teachings of (late) Dr. John Cherry I, Bishop TD Jakes, (late) Dr. Myles Munroe, Pastor Joseph Prince, Pastor Joel Osteen, Rev. Joyce Myers, and Dr. Tony Evans. His lifetime heroes include his parents, siblings, and many others whom he believes are major contributors to the body of Christ.

He lives in Maryland, outside of DC, and is bi-vocational in education and ministry. He's the proud founder/senior leader of Redeemed Christian Worship Center. His desire in writing this book is to inspire people to join the movement of forgiveness!

CPSIA information can be obtained
at www.ICGtesting.com
Printed in the USA
FSHW011319010720
71531FS

9 781640 888968